MznLnx

Missing Links Exam Preps

Exam Prep for

New Products Management

Crawford & Benedetto, 9th Edition

The MznLnx Exam Prep is your link from the texbook and lecture to your exams.
The MznLnx Exam Preps are unauthorized and comprehensive reviews of your textbooks.

All material provided by MznLnx and Rico Publications (c) 2010
Textbook publishers and textbook authors do not particpate in or contribute to these reviews.

MznLnx

Rico
Publications

Exam Prep for New Products Management
9th Edition
Crawford & Benedetto

Publisher: Raymond Houge
Assistant Editor: Michael Rouger
Text and Cover Designer: Lisa Buckner
Marketing Manager: Sara Swagger
Project Manager, Editorial Production: Jerry Emerson
Art Director: Vernon Lowerui

Product Manager: Dave Mason
Editorial Assitant: Rachel Guzmanji
Pedagogy: Debra Long
Cover Image: Jim Reed/Getty Images
Text and Cover Printer: City Printing, Inc.
Compositor: Media Mix, Inc.

(c) 2010 Rico Publications
ALL RIGHTS RESERVED. No part of this work covered by the copyright may be reproduced or used in any form or by an means--graphic, electronic, or mechanical, including photocopying, recording, taping, Web distribution, information storage, and retrieval systems, or in any other manner--without the written permission of the publisher.

For more information about our products, contact us at:
Dave.Mason@RicoPublications.com

For permission to use material from this text or product, submit a request online to:
Dave.Mason@RicoPublications.com

Printed in the United States
ISBN:

Contents

CHAPTER 1
The Menu — 1

CHAPTER 2
The New Products Process — 10

CHAPTER 3
Opportunity Identification and Selection: Strategic Planning for New Products — 20

CHAPTER 4
Preparation and Alternatives — 28

CHAPTER 5
Problem-Based Ideation: Finding and Solving Customers' Problems — 33

CHAPTER 6
Analytical Attribute Approaches: Introduction and Perceptual Mapping — 36

CHAPTER 7
Analytical Attribute Approaches: Trade-off Analysis and Qualitative Techniques — 39

CHAPTER 8
The Concept Evaluation System — 42

CHAPTER 9
Concept Testing — 47

CHAPTER 10
The Full Screen — 51

CHAPTER 11
Sales Forecasting and Financial Analysis — 54

CHAPTER 12
Product Protocol — 61

CHAPTER 13
Design — 64

CHAPTER 14
Development Team Management — 68

CHAPTER 15
Product Use Testing — 76

CHAPTER 16
Strategic Launch Planning — 80

CHAPTER 17
Implementation of the Strategic Plan — 88

CHAPTER 18
Market Testing — 90

CHAPTER 19
Launch Management — 96

CHAPTER 20
Public Policy Issues — 99

ANSWER KEY — 110

TO THE STUDENT

COMPREHENSIVE

The *MznLnx* Exam Prep series is designed to help you pass your exams. Editors at MznLnx review your textbooks and then prepare these practice exams to help you master the textbook material. Unlike study guides, workbooks, and practice tests provided by the texbook publisher and textbook authors, *MznLnx* gives you **all** of the material in each chapter in exam form, not just samples, so you can be sure to nail your exam.

MECHANICAL

The MznLnx Exam Prep series creates exams that will help you learn the subject matter as well as test you on your understanding. Each question is designed to help you master the concept. Just working through the exams, you gain an understanding of the subject--its a simple mechanical process that produces success.

INTEGRATED STUDY GUIDE AND REVIEW

MznLnx is not just a set of exams designed to test you, its also a comprehensive review of the subject content. Each exam question is also a review of the concept, making sure that you will get the answer correct without having to go to other sources of material. You learn as you go! Its the easiest way to pass an exam.

HUMOR

Studying can be tedious and dry. MznLnx's instructional design includes moderate humor within the exam questions on occassion, to break the tedium and revitalize the brain

Chapter 1. The Menu

1. In marketing, _____ has come to mean the process by which marketers try to create an image or identity in the minds of their target market for its product, brand, or organization. It is the 'relative competitive comparison' their product occupies in a given market as perceived by the target market.

Re-_____ involves changing the identity of a product, relative to the identity of competing products, in the collective minds of the target market.

   a. Context analysis
   b. Customer analytics
   c. Positioning
   d. PEST analysis

2. The process of _____ involves the introduction of a good or service that is new or substantially improved. This includes, but is not limited to, improvements in functional characteristics, technical abilities, or ease of use.
   a. Product innovation
   b. Service-profit chain
   c. Letter of resignation
   d. Job enlargement

3. _____ is the frequency with which an engineered system or component fails, expressed for example in failures per hour. It is often denoted by the Greek letter >λ and is important in reliability theory.

The _____ of a system usually depends on time, with the rate varying over the life cycle of the system.

   a. Heteroskedastic
   b. Statistics
   c. Correlation
   d. Failure rate

4. _____ in its literal sense is the process of transformation of local or regional phenomena into global ones. It can be described as a process by which the people of the world are unified into a single society and function together.

This process is a combination of economic, technological, sociocultural and political forces.

   a. Histogram
   b. Globalization
   c. Collaborative Planning, Forecasting and Replenishment
   d. Cost Management

5. _____ is a civil designation for persons who are incorporated in a fixed or permanent way to a society or group: regular member of the working staff, permanent staff distinguished from a supernumerary.

The term '_____' and its counterpart, 'supernumerary,' originated in Spanish and Latin American academy and government; it is now also used in countries all over the world, such as France, the U.S., England, Italy, etc.

There are _____ members of surgical organizations, of universities, of gastronomical associations, etc.

   a. Adam Smith
   b. Affiliation
   c. Numerary
   d. Abraham Harold Maslow

6. The _____ captures an expanded spectrum of values and criteria for measuring organizational success: economic, ecological and social. With the ratification of the United Nations and ICLEI _____ standard for urban and community accounting in early 2007, this became the dominant approach to public sector full cost accounting. Similar UN standards apply to natural capital and human capital measurement to assist in measurements required by _____, e.g. the ecoBudget standard for reporting ecological footprint.
   a. 33 Strategies of War
   b. Triple bottom line
   c. 28-hour day
   d. 1990 Clean Air Act

7. _____ is an adjective for experience-based techniques that help in problem solving, learning and discovery. A _____ method is particularly used to rapidly come to a solution that is hoped to be close to the best possible answer, or 'optimal solution'. _____s are 'rules of thumb', educated guesses, intuitive judgments or simply common sense.
   a. Representativeness
   b. 1990 Clean Air Act
   c. 28-hour day
   d. Heuristic

Chapter 1. The Menu

8. _____ refers to the movement of cash into or out of a business or financial product. It is usually measured during a specified, finite period of time. Measurement of _____ can be used

- to determine a project's rate of return or value. The time of _____s into and out of projects are used as inputs in financial models such as internal rate of return, and net present value.
- to determine problems with a business's liquidity. Being profitable does not necessarily mean being liquid. A company can fail because of a shortage of cash, even while profitable.
- as an alternate measure of a business's profits when it is believed that accrual accounting concepts do not represent economic realities. For example, a company may be notionally profitable but generating little operational cash (as may be the case for a company that barters its products rather than selling for cash.) In such a case, the company may be deriving additional operating cash by issuing shares evaluating default risk, re-investment requirements, etc.

_____ is a generic term used differently depending on the context. It may be defined by users for their own purposes.

a. Cash flow
b. Sweat equity
c. Gross profit margin
d. Gross profit

9. In business and engineering, new _____ is the term used to describe the complete process of bringing a new product or service to market. There are two parallel paths involved in the NProduct development process: one involves the idea generation, product design, and detail engineering; the other involves market research and marketing analysis. Companies typically see new _____ as the first stage in generating and commercializing new products within the overall strategic process of product life cycle management used to maintain or grow their market share.

a. 33 Strategies of War
b. Product development
c. 28-hour day
d. 1990 Clean Air Act

10. In economics, business, retail, and accounting, a _____ is the value of money that has been used up to produce something, and hence is not available for use anymore. In economics, a _____ is an alternative that is given up as a result of a decision. In business, the _____ may be one of acquisition, in which case the amount of money expended to acquire it is counted as _____.

a. Cost allocation
b. Cost
c. Fixed costs
d. Cost overrun

11. There are many important decisions about product and service development and marketing. In the process of product development and marketing we should focus on strategic decisions about product attributes, product branding, product packaging, product labeling and product support services. But product strategy also calls for building a _____.
   a. Marketing strategy
   b. Context analysis
   c. Product bundling
   d. Product line

12. _____ is a broad label that refers to any individuals or households that use goods and services generated within the economy. The concept of a _____ is used in different contexts, so that the usage and significance of the term may vary.

Typically when business people and economists talk of _____s they are talking about person as _____, an aggregated commodity item with little individuality other than that expressed in the buy/not-buy decision.

   a. Consumer
   b. 1990 Clean Air Act
   c. 33 Strategies of War
   d. 28-hour day

13. In decision theory and estimation theory, the _____ of an estimator, $\hat{\theta}$, of an unknown parameter of the distribution, θ, is the expected value of the loss function

$$R(\theta, \hat{\theta}) = \mathbb{E}_\theta L(\theta, \hat{\theta}) = \int L(\theta, \hat{\theta})\, dP_\theta.$$

where dP_θ is a probability measure parametrized by θ.

- For a scalar parameter θ and a quadratic loss function,

$$L(\theta, \hat{\theta}) = (\theta - \hat{\theta})^2$$

the _____ function becomes the mean squared error of the estimate,

$$R(\theta, \hat{\theta}) = E_\theta (\theta - \hat{\theta})^2$$

- In density estimation, the unknown parameter is probability density itself. The loss function is typically chosen to be a norm in an appropriate function space. For example, for L^2 norm,

$$L(f, \hat{f}) = \|f - \hat{f}\|_2^2$$

the _____ function becomes the mean integrated squared error

$$R(f, \hat{f}) = E\|f - \hat{f}\|^2$$

a. Risk aversion
b. Financial modeling
c. Linear model
d. Risk

14. _____ describes commerce transactions between businesses, such as between a manufacturer and a wholesaler, or between a wholesaler and a retailer. Contrasting terms are business-to-consumer (B2C) and business-to-government (B2G.)

The volume of B2B transactions is much higher than the volume of B2C transactions.

a. Category management
b. Market environment
c. Product bundling
d. Business-to-business

15. _____ is an advertisement in which a particular product specifically mentions a competitor by name for the express purpose of showing why the competitor is inferior to the product naming it.

This should not be confused with parody advertisements, where a fictional product is being advertised for the purpose of poking fun at the particular advertisement, nor should it be confused with the use of a coined brand name for the purpose of comparing the product without actually naming an actual competitor. ('Wikipedia tastes better and is less filling than the Encyclopedia Galactica.')

In the 1980s, during what has been referred to as the cola wars, soft-drink manufacturer Pepsi ran a series of advertisements where people, caught on hidden camera, in a blind taste test, chose Pepsi over rival Coca-Cola.

   a. 1990 Clean Air Act
   b. 28-hour day
   c. 33 Strategies of War
   d. Comparative advertising

16. _____ refers to the difference between the cost of materials purchased by a company plus the cost of the labor to assemble a product and the price at which the company sells the product. An example is the price of gasoline at the pump over the price of the oil in it. In national accounts used in macroeconomics, it refers to the contribution of the factors of production, i.e., land, labor, and capital goods, to raising the value of a product and corresponds to the incomes received by the owners of these factors.
   a. Value added
   b. Deregulation
   c. Rehn-Meidner Model
   d. Minimum wage

17. _____ is the area of law in which manufacturers, distributors, suppliers, retailers, and others who make products available to the public are held responsible for the injuries those products cause.

In the United States, the claims most commonly associated with _____ are negligence, strict liability, breach of warranty, and various consumer protection claims. The majority of _____ laws are determined at the state level and vary widely from state to state.

   a. Product liability
   b. Right-to-work laws
   c. Railway Labor Act
   d. Leave of absence

18. In business and engineering, _____ is the term used to describe the complete process of bringing a new product or service to market. There are two parallel paths involved in the _____ process: one involves the idea generation, product design, and detail engineering; the other involves market research and marketing analysis. Companies typically see _____ as the first stage in generating and commercializing new products within the overall strategic process of product life cycle management used to maintain or grow their market share.

   a. 1990 Clean Air Act
   b. New product development
   c. 33 Strategies of War
   d. 28-hour day

19. In economics, _____ is the desire to own something and the ability to pay for it. The term _____ signifies the ability or the willingness to buy a particular commodity at a given point of time.

   a. Demand
   b. 33 Strategies of War
   c. 28-hour day
   d. 1990 Clean Air Act

20. _____ is an integrated communications-based process through which individuals and communities discover that existing and newly-identified needs and wants may be satisfied by the products and services of others.

   _____ is defined by the American _____ Association as the activity, set of institutions, and processes for creating, communicating, delivering, and exchanging offerings that have value for customers, clients, partners, and society at large. The term developed from the original meaning which referred literally to going to market, as in shopping, or going to a market to buy or sell goods or services.

   a. Marketing
   b. Market development
   c. Disruptive technology
   d. Customer relationship management

21. _____ is a term defined by the Oxford English Dictionary as an individual's 'course or progress through life '. It is usually considered to pertain to remunerative work (and sometimes also formal education.)

The etymology of the term is somewhat ironic in that it comes from the Latin word carrera, which means race .

a. Career planning
b. Nursing shortage
c. Career
d. Spatial mismatch

22. _____ can be defined as the idea generation, concept development, testing and manufacturing or implementation of a physical object or service. _____ers conceptualize and evaluate ideas, making them tangible through products in a more systematic approach. The role of a _____er encompasses many characteristics of the marketing manager, product manager, industrial designer and design engineer.
   a. Abraham Harold Maslow
   b. Affiliation
   c. Adam Smith
   d. Product design

23. A _____ is a professional in the field of project management. _____s can have the responsibility of the planning, execution, and closing of any project, typically relating to construction industry, architecture, computer networking, telecommunications or software development.

Many other fields in the production, design and service industries also have _____s.

   a. Project engineer
   b. Work package
   c. Project management
   d. Project manager

24. _____ is the discipline of managing processes in research and development (R'D) and innovation. It can be used to develop both product and organizational innovation. Without proper processes, it is not possible for R'D to be efficient; _____ includes a set of tools that allow managers and engineers to cooperate with a common understanding of goals and processes.
   a. A4e
   b. AAAI
   c. Innovation Management
   d. A Stake in the Outcome

25. A _____ is typically described as a deliberate plan of action to guide decisions and achieve rational outcome(s). However, the term may also be used to denote what is actually done, even though it is unplanned.

The term may apply to government, private sector organizations and groups, and individuals.

a. 1990 Clean Air Act
b. 28-hour day
c. Policy
d. 33 Strategies of War

Chapter 2. The New Products Process

1. _____ is an integrated communications-based process through which individuals and communities discover that existing and newly-identified needs and wants may be satisfied by the products and services of others.

   _____ is defined by the American _____ Association as the activity, set of institutions, and processes for creating, communicating, delivering, and exchanging offerings that have value for customers, clients, partners, and society at large. The term developed from the original meaning which referred literally to going to market, as in shopping, or going to a market to buy or sell goods or services.

   a. Customer relationship management
   b. Marketing
   c. Market development
   d. Disruptive technology

2. A _____ is a group of employees from various functional areas of the organization - research, engineering, marketing, finance. human resources, and operations, for example - who are all focused on a specific objective and are responsible to work as a team to improve coordination and innovation across divisions and resolve mutual problems.

   a. Goal-setting theory
   b. Sociotechnical systems
   c. Cross-functional team
   d. Graduate recruitment

3. _____ is an organization's process of defining its strategy and making decisions on allocating its resources to pursue this strategy, including its capital and people. Various business analysis techniques can be used in _____, including SWOT analysis (Strengths, Weaknesses, Opportunities, and Threats) and PEST analysis (Political, Economic, Social, and Technological analysis) or STEER analysis involving Socio-cultural, Technological, Economic, Ecological, and Regulatory factors and EPISTEL (Environment, Political, Informatic, Social, Technological, Economic and Legal)

   _____ is the formal consideration of an organization's future course. All _____ deals with at least one of three key questions:

   1. 'What do we do?'
   2. 'For whom do we do it?'
   3. 'How do we excel?'

   In business _____, the third question is better phrased 'How can we beat or avoid competition?'. (Bradford and Duncan, page 1.)

Chapter 2. The New Products Process

a. Strategic planning
b. 28-hour day
c. 33 Strategies of War
d. 1990 Clean Air Act

4. In commerce, _____ is the length of time it takes from a product being conceived until its being available for sale. _____ is important in industries where products are outmoded quickly. A common assumption is that _____ matters most for first-of-a-kind products, but actually the leader often has the luxury of time, while the clock is clearly running for the followers.
   a. Market entry
   b. Procurement
   c. Time to market
   d. Career development

5. In physics, and more specifically kinematics, _____ is the change in velocity over time. Because velocity is a vector, it can change in two ways: a change in magnitude and/or a change in direction. In one dimension, _____ is the rate at which something speeds up or slows down.
   a. A4e
   b. AAAI
   c. A Stake in the Outcome
   d. Acceleration

6. In business and engineering, new _____ is the term used to describe the complete process of bringing a new product or service to market. There are two parallel paths involved in the NProduct development process: one involves the idea generation, product design, and detail engineering; the other involves market research and marketing analysis. Companies typically see new _____ as the first stage in generating and commercializing new products within the overall strategic process of product life cycle management used to maintain or grow their market share.
   a. 1990 Clean Air Act
   b. 33 Strategies of War
   c. 28-hour day
   d. Product development

7. The process of _____ involves the introduction of a good or service that is new or substantially improved. This includes, but is not limited to, improvements in functional characteristics, technical abilities, or ease of use.

a. Job enlargement
b. Service-profit chain
c. Letter of resignation
d. Product innovation

8. _____ refers to the movement of cash into or out of a business or financial product. It is usually measured during a specified, finite period of time. Measurement of _____ can be used

- to determine a project's rate of return or value. The time of _____s into and out of projects are used as inputs in financial models such as internal rate of return, and net present value.
- to determine problems with a business's liquidity. Being profitable does not necessarily mean being liquid. A company can fail because of a shortage of cash, even while profitable.
- as an alternate measure of a business's profits when it is believed that accrual accounting concepts do not represent economic realities. For example, a company may be notionally profitable but generating little operational cash (as may be the case for a company that barters its products rather than selling for cash.) In such a case, the company may be deriving additional operating cash by issuing shares evaluating default risk, re-investment requirements, etc.

_____ is a generic term used differently depending on the context. It may be defined by users for their own purposes.

a. Gross profit
b. Gross profit margin
c. Sweat equity
d. Cash flow

9. _____ is a 'method to transform user demands into design quality, to deploy the functions forming quality, and to deploy methods for achieving the design quality into subsystems and component parts, and ultimately to specific elements of the manufacturing process.' , as described by Dr. Yoji Akao, who originally developed _____ in Japan in 1966, when the author combined his work in quality assurance and quality control points with function deployment used in Value Engineering.

_____ is designed to help planners focus on characteristics of a new or existing product or service from the viewpoints of market segments, company, or technology-development needs. The technique yields graphs and matrices.

a. Hoshin Kanri
b. 1990 Clean Air Act
c. Learning organization
d. Quality function deployment

10. A _____ is a written document that details the necessary actions to achieve one or more marketing objectives. It can be for a product or service, a brand, or a product line. _____s cover between one and five years.
   a. Market development
   b. Disruptive technology
   c. Marketing plan
   d. Marketing strategy

11. _____ is the set of tasks, knowledge, and techniques required to identify business needs and determine solutions to business problems. Solutions often include a systems development component, but may also consist of process improvement or organizational change. The person who carries out this task is called a business analyst or _____.
   a. Door-to-door selling
   b. 28-hour day
   c. Business analysis
   d. 1990 Clean Air Act

12. A _____, in the field of business and marketing, is a geographic region or demographic group used to gauge the viability of a product or service in the mass market prior to a wide scale roll-out. The criteria used to judge the acceptability of a _____ region or group include:

   1. a population that is demographically similar to the proposed target market; and
   2. relative isolation from densely populated media markets so that advertising to the test audience can be efficient and economical.

The _____ ideally aims to duplicate 'everything' - promotion and distribution as well as `product' - on a smaller scale. The technique replicates, typically in one area, what is planned to occur in a national launch; and the results are very carefully monitored, so that they can be extrapolated to projected national results. The `area' may be any one of the following:

- Television area

internet online test

- Test town
- Residential neighborhood
- Test site

A number of decisions have to be taken about any _____:

- Which _____?
- What is to be tested?
- How long a test?
- What are the success criteria?

The simple go or no-go decision, together with the related reduction of risk, is normally the main justification for the expense of _____s. At the same time, however, such _____s can be used to test specific elements of a new product's marketing mix; possibly the version of the product itself, the promotional message and media spend, the distribution channels and the price.

    a. 33 Strategies of War
    b. 1990 Clean Air Act
    c. 28-hour day
    d. Test market

13. _____ is one of the main objectives of advertising and promotion. When people think of examples of a product type or category, they usually think of a limited number of brand names. For example, a prospective buyer of a college education will have several thousand colleges to choose from.
    a. 28-hour day
    b. 33 Strategies of War
    c. 1990 Clean Air Act
    d. Mind share

14. _____ is an area of knowledge within organizational theory that studies models and theories about the way an organization learns and adapts.

In Organizational development (OD), learning is a characteristic of an adaptive organization, i.e., an organization that is able to sense changes in signals from its environment (both internal and external) and adapt accordingly.

    a. A4e
    b. AAAI
    c. A Stake in the Outcome
    d. Organizational learning

15. A _____ is a process in which a potential employee is evaluated by an employer for prospective employment in their company, organization and was established in the late 16th century.

A _____ typically precedes the hiring decision, and is used to evaluate the candidate. The interview is usually preceded by the evaluation of submitted résumés from interested candidates, then selecting a small number of candidates for interviews.

   a. Payrolling
   b. Supported employment
   c. Job interview
   d. Split shift

16. A _____ is a formal relationship between two or more parties to pursue a set of agreed upon goals or to meet a critical business need while remaining independent organizations.

Partners may provide the _____ with resources such as products, distribution channels, manufacturing capability, project funding, capital equipment, knowledge, expertise, or intellectual property. The alliance is a cooperation or collaboration which aims for a synergy where each partner hopes that the benefits from the alliance will be greater than those from individual efforts.

   a. Strategic alliance
   b. Farmshoring
   c. Process automation
   d. Golden parachute

17. The _____ captures an expanded spectrum of values and criteria for measuring organizational success: economic, ecological and social. With the ratification of the United Nations and ICLEI _____ standard for urban and community accounting in early 2007, this became the dominant approach to public sector full cost accounting. Similar UN standards apply to natural capital and human capital measurement to assist in measurements required by _____, e.g. the ecoBudget standard for reporting ecological footprint.
   a. 28-hour day
   b. 33 Strategies of War
   c. 1990 Clean Air Act
   d. Triple bottom line

18. In decision theory and estimation theory, the _____ of an estimator, $\hat{\theta}$, of an unknown parameter of the distribution, θ, is the expected value of the loss function

$$R(\theta, \hat{\theta}) = \mathbb{E}_\theta L(\theta, \hat{\theta}) = \int L(\theta, \hat{\theta})\, dP_\theta.$$

where dP_θ is a probability measure parametrized by θ.

- For a scalar parameter θ and a quadratic loss function,

$$L(\theta, \hat{\theta}) = (\theta - \hat{\theta})^2$$

the _____ function becomes the mean squared error of the estimate,

$$R(\theta, \hat{\theta}) = E_\theta(\theta - \hat{\theta})^2$$

- In density estimation, the unknown parameter is probability density itself. The loss function is typically chosen to be a norm in an appropriate function space. For example, for L^2 norm,

$$L(f, \hat{f}) = \|f - \hat{f}\|_2^2$$

the _____ function becomes the mean integrated squared error

$$R(f, \hat{f}) = E\|f - \hat{f}\|^2$$

a. Financial modeling
b. Risk aversion
c. Risk
d. Linear model

19. _____ is an advertisement in which a particular product specifically mentions a competitor by name for the express purpose of showing why the competitor is inferior to the product naming it.

This should not be confused with parody advertisements, where a fictional product is being advertised for the purpose of poking fun at the particular advertisement, nor should it be confused with the use of a coined brand name for the purpose of comparing the product without actually naming an actual competitor. ('Wikipedia tastes better and is less filling than the Encyclopedia Galactica.')

In the 1980s, during what has been referred to as the cola wars, soft-drink manufacturer Pepsi ran a series of advertisements where people, caught on hidden camera, in a blind taste test, chose Pepsi over rival Coca-Cola.

a. Comparative advertising
b. 1990 Clean Air Act
c. 33 Strategies of War
d. 28-hour day

20. A _____ is directly responsible for managing the day-to-day operations (and profitability) of a company.

Chief Executive Officer (CEO)
   - As the top manager, the CEO is typically responsible for the entire operations of the corporation and reports directly to the chairman and board of directors. It is the CEO's responsibility to implement board decisions and initiatives and to maintain the smooth operation of the firm, with the assistance of senior management.

a. Field service management
b. Management team
c. Getting Things Done
d. Vorstand

21. _____ is a process of planning and controlling the performance or execution of any type of activity, such as:

- a project (project _____) or
- a process (process _____, sometimes referred to as the process performance measurement and management system.)

Organization's senior management is responsible for carrying out its _____.

a. Work design
b. Participatory management
c. Management process
d. Human Relations Movement

22. _____ is a civil designation for persons who are incorporated in a fixed or permanent way to a society or group: regular member of the working staff, permanent staff distinguished from a supernumerary.

The term '_____' and its counterpart, 'supernumerary,' originated in Spanish and Latin American academy and government; it is now also used in countries all over the world, such as France, the U.S., England, Italy, etc.

There are _____ members of surgical organizations, of universities, of gastronomical associations, etc.

a. Adam Smith
b. Abraham Harold Maslow
c. Numerary
d. Affiliation

23. _____ is a term developed by Eric von Hippel in 1986. His definition for _____ is:

   1. _____s face needs that will be general in a marketplace - but face them months or years before the bulk of that marketplace encounters them, and
   2. _____s are positioned to benefit significantly by obtaining a solution to those needs.

In other words: _____s are users of a product that currently experience needs still unknown to the public and who also benefit greatly if they obtain a solution to these needs.

The _____ Method is a market research tool that may be used by companies and / or individuals seeking to develop breakthrough products. _____ methodology was originally developed by Dr. Eric von Hippel of the Massachusetts Institute of Technology (MIT) and first described in the July 1986 issue of the Journal of Management Science.

   a. 33 Strategies of War
   b. 1990 Clean Air Act
   c. 28-hour day
   d. Lead user

24. _____ is a term used in business and Information Technology (through ITIL) to describe the process of capturing a customer's requirements. Specifically, the _____ is a market research technique that produces a detailed set of customer wants and needs, organized into a hierarchical structure, and then prioritized in terms of relative importance and satisfaction with current alternatives. _____ studies typically consist of both qualitative and quantitative research steps.
   a. Goal setting
   b. Business philosophy
   c. Board of governors
   d. Voice of the customer

25. In probability theory, a probability distribution is called _____ if its cumulative distribution function is _____. This is equivalent to saying that for random variables X with the distribution in question, Pr[X = a] = 0 for all real numbers a, i.e.: the probability that X attains the value a is zero, for any number a. If the distribution of X is _____ then X is called a _____ random variable.

a. Pay Band
b. Continuous
c. Connectionist expert systems
d. Decision tree pruning

Chapter 3. Opportunity Identification and Selection: Strategic Planning for New Products

1. _____ is an organization's process of defining its strategy and making decisions on allocating its resources to pursue this strategy, including its capital and people. Various business analysis techniques can be used in _____, including SWOT analysis (Strengths, Weaknesses, Opportunities, and Threats) and PEST analysis (Political, Economic, Social, and Technological analysis) or STEER analysis involving Socio-cultural, Technological, Economic, Ecological, and Regulatory factors and EPISTEL (Environment, Political, Informatic, Social, Technological, Economic and Legal)

_____ is the formal consideration of an organization's future course. All _____ deals with at least one of three key questions:

   1. 'What do we do?'
   2. 'For whom do we do it?'
   3. 'How do we excel?'

In business _____, the third question is better phrased 'How can we beat or avoid competition?'. (Bradford and Duncan, page 1.)

   a. 33 Strategies of War
   b. Strategic planning
   c. 1990 Clean Air Act
   d. 28-hour day

2. The process of _____ involves the introduction of a good or service that is new or substantially improved. This includes, but is not limited to, improvements in functional characteristics, technical abilities, or ease of use.
   a. Letter of resignation
   b. Product innovation
   c. Service-profit chain
   d. Job enlargement

3. _____ is the state or fact of exclusive rights and control over property, which may be an object, land/real estate or intellectual property. An _____ right is also referred to as title. The concept of _____ has existed for thousands of years and in all cultures.
   a. A4e
   b. A Stake in the Outcome
   c. Emanation of the state
   d. Ownership

4. A _____ is a brief written statement of the purpose of a company or organization. Ideally, a _____ guides the actions of the organization, spells out its overall goal, provides a sense of direction, and guides decision making for all levels of management.

Chapter 3. Opportunity Identification and Selection: Strategic Planning for New Products

_____s often contain the following:

- Purpose and aim of the organization
- The organization's primary stakeholders: clients, stockholders, etc.
- Responsibilities of the organization toward these stakeholders
- Products and services offered

In developing a _____:

- Encourage as much input as feasible from employees, volunteers, and other stakeholders
- Publicize it broadly

The _____ can be used to resolve differences between business stakeholders. Stakeholders include: employees including managers and executives, stockholders, board of directors, customers, suppliers, distributors, creditors, governments (local, state, federal, etc.), unions, competitors, NGO's, and the general public.

a. 1990 Clean Air Act
b. Mission statement
c. 33 Strategies of War
d. 28-hour day

5. A _____ is a name or trademark connected with a product or producer. _____s have become increasingly important components of culture and the economy, now being described as 'cultural accessories and personal philosophies'.

Some people distinguish the psychological aspect of a _____ from the experiential aspect.

a. Brand awareness
b. Brand loyalty
c. Brand extension
d. Brand

6. A _____ is a formal relationship between two or more parties to pursue a set of agreed upon goals or to meet a critical business need while remaining independent organizations.

Partners may provide the _____ with resources such as products, distribution channels, manufacturing capability, project funding, capital equipment, knowledge, expertise, or intellectual property. The alliance is a cooperation or collaboration which aims for a synergy where each partner hopes that the benefits from the alliance will be greater than those from individual efforts.

Chapter 3. Opportunity Identification and Selection: Strategic Planning for New Products

a. Farmshoring
b. Golden parachute
c. Process automation
d. Strategic alliance

7. In economics, _____ is a measure of the relative satisfaction from consumption of various goods and services. Given this measure, one may speak meaningfully of increasing or decreasing _____, and thereby explain economic behavior in terms of attempts to increase one's _____. For illustrative purposes, changes in _____ are sometimes expressed in units called utils.

a. Indirect utility function
b. Ordinal utility
c. A Stake in the Outcome
d. Utility

8. _____ is understood as a business unit within the overall corporate identity which is distinguishable from other business because it serves a defined external market where management can conduct strategic planning in relation to products and markets. When companies become really large, they are best thought of as being composed of a number of businesses (or _____s.)

In the broader domain of strategic management, the phrase '_____' came into use in the 1960s, largely as a result of General Electric's many units.

a. Strategic group
b. Switching cost
c. Strategic business unit
d. Strategic drift

9. _____ is a statistical technique that originated in mathematical psychology. Today it is used in many of the social sciences and applied sciences including marketing, product management, and operations research. It is not to be confused with the theory of conjoint measurement.

a. Classical test theory
b. Conjoint analysis
c. Semantic differential
d. Counternull

10. _____, a business term, is a measure of how products and services supplied by a company meet or surpass customer expectation. It is seen as a key performance indicator within business and is part of the four perspectives of a Balanced Scorecard.

Chapter 3. Opportunity Identification and Selection: Strategic Planning for New Products

In a competitive marketplace where businesses compete for customers, _____ is seen as a key differentiator and increasingly has become a key element of business strategy.

a. Critical Success Factor
b. Foreign ownership
c. Horizontal integration
d. Customer satisfaction

11. A _____ is a process in which a potential employee is evaluated by an employer for prospective employment in their company, organization and was established in the late 16th century.

A _____ typically precedes the hiring decision, and is used to evaluate the candidate. The interview is usually preceded by the evaluation of submitted résumés from interested candidates, then selecting a small number of candidates for interviews.

a. Job interview
b. Payrolling
c. Split shift
d. Supported employment

12. _____ is the corporate management term for the act of reorganizing the legal, ownership, operational, or other structures of a company for the purpose of making it more profitable, or better organized for its present needs. Alternate reasons for _____ include a change of ownership or ownership structure, demerger repositioning debt _____ and financial _____.

a. Market value
b. Net worth
c. Market value added
d. Restructuring

13. In decision theory and estimation theory, the _____ of an estimator, $\hat{\theta}$, of an unknown parameter of the distribution, θ, is the expected value of the loss function

$$R(\theta, \hat{\theta}) = \mathbb{E}_\theta L(\theta, \hat{\theta}) = \int L(\theta, \hat{\theta})\, dP_\theta.$$

Chapter 3. Opportunity Identification and Selection: Strategic Planning for New Products

where dP_θ is a probability measure parametrized by θ.

- For a scalar parameter θ and a quadratic loss function,

$$L(\theta, \hat{\theta}) = (\theta - \hat{\theta})^2$$

the _____ function becomes the mean squared error of the estimate,

$$R(\theta, \hat{\theta}) = E_\theta (\theta - \hat{\theta})^2$$

- In density estimation, the unknown parameter is probability density itself. The loss function is typically chosen to be a norm in an appropriate function space. For example, for L^2 norm,

$$L(f, \hat{f}) = \|f - \hat{f}\|_2^2$$

the _____ function becomes the mean integrated squared error

$$R(f, \hat{f}) = E\|f - \hat{f}\|^2$$

a. Risk
b. Risk aversion
c. Financial modeling
d. Linear model

14. The phrase mergers and _____s refers to the aspect of corporate strategy, corporate finance and management dealing with the buying, selling and combining of different companies that can aid, finance, or help a growing company in a given industry grow rapidly without having to create another business entity.

An _____, also known as a takeover or a buyout, is the buying of one company (the 'target') by another. An _____ may be friendly or hostile.

a. A4e
b. AAAI
c. A Stake in the Outcome
d. Acquisition

Chapter 3. Opportunity Identification and Selection: Strategic Planning for New Products

15. _____ is something that a firm can do well and that meets the following three conditions:

Competencies are things that companys execute well across several business units or product sectors.

Firms usually have few competencies, but these are usually less liable to change rapidly.

1. It provides consumer benefits
2. It is not easy for competitors to imitate
3. It can be leveraged widely to many products and markets.

A _____ can take various forms, including technical/subject matter know-how, a reliable process and/or close relationships with customers and suppliers (Mascarenhas et al. 1998.)

a. NAIRU
b. Learning-by-doing
c. Dominant Design
d. Core competency

16. While the full name of the Swiss verein is Deloitte Touche Tohmatsu, in 1989 it initially branded itself _____ and then simply Deloitte. In 2003 the rebranding campaign was commissioned by Bill Parrett, the then CEO of DTT, and led by Jerry Leamon, the global Clients and Markets leader.

Deloitte member firms offer services in the following functions, with country-specific variations on their legal implementation (i.e. all operating within a single company or through separate legal entities operating as subsidiaries of an umbrella legal entity for the country.)

a. 33 Strategies of War
b. 28-hour day
c. 1990 Clean Air Act
d. Deloitte ' Touche

17. _____ is an integrated communications-based process through which individuals and communities discover that existing and newly-identified needs and wants may be satisfied by the products and services of others.

_____ is defined by the American _____ Association as the activity, set of institutions, and processes for creating, communicating, delivering, and exchanging offerings that have value for customers, clients, partners, and society at large. The term developed from the original meaning which referred literally to going to market, as in shopping, or going to a market to buy or sell goods or services.

26 Chapter 3. Opportunity Identification and Selection: Strategic Planning for New Products

a. Disruptive technology
b. Customer relationship management
c. Marketing
d. Market development

18. In physics, and more specifically kinematics, _____ is the change in velocity over time. Because velocity is a vector, it can change in two ways: a change in magnitude and/or a change in direction. In one dimension, _____ is the rate at which something speeds up or slows down.

a. AAAI
b. A Stake in the Outcome
c. A4e
d. Acceleration

19. _____, in marketing, manufacturing, call centres and management, is the use of flexible computer-aided manufacturing systems to produce custom output. Those systems combine the low unit costs of mass production processes with the flexibility of individual customization.

'_____' is the new frontier in business competition for both manufacturing and service industries.

a. 28-hour day
b. 1990 Clean Air Act
c. 33 Strategies of War
d. Mass customization

20. _____ is an advertisement in which a particular product specifically mentions a competitor by name for the express purpose of showing why the competitor is inferior to the product naming it.

This should not be confused with parody advertisements, where a fictional product is being advertised for the purpose of poking fun at the particular advertisement, nor should it be confused with the use of a coined brand name for the purpose of comparing the product without actually naming an actual competitor. ('Wikipedia tastes better and is less filling than the Encyclopedia Galactica.')

In the 1980s, during what has been referred to as the cola wars, soft-drink manufacturer Pepsi ran a series of advertisements where people, caught on hidden camera, in a blind taste test, chose Pepsi over rival Coca-Cola.

Chapter 3. Opportunity Identification and Selection: Strategic Planning for New Products 27

a. 1990 Clean Air Act
b. Comparative advertising
c. 28-hour day
d. 33 Strategies of War

21. _____ is the discipline of managing processes in research and development (R'D) and innovation. It can be used to develop both product and organizational innovation. Without proper processes, it is not possible for R'D to be efficient; _____ includes a set of tools that allow managers and engineers to cooperate with a common understanding of goals and processes.
    a. A Stake in the Outcome
    b. A4e
    c. AAAI
    d. Innovation management

22. The _____ captures an expanded spectrum of values and criteria for measuring organizational success: economic, ecological and social. With the ratification of the United Nations and ICLEI _____ standard for urban and community accounting in early 2007, this became the dominant approach to public sector full cost accounting. Similar UN standards apply to natural capital and human capital measurement to assist in measurements required by _____, e.g. the ecoBudget standard for reporting ecological footprint.
    a. Triple bottom line
    b. 33 Strategies of War
    c. 1990 Clean Air Act
    d. 28-hour day

Chapter 4. Preparation and Alternatives

1. The _____ assessment is a psychometric questionnaire designed to measure psychological preferences in how people perceive the world and make decisions.[1] These preferences were extrapolated from the typological theories originated by Carl Gustav Jung, as published in his 1921 book Psychological Types. The original developers of the personality inventory were Katharine Cook Briggs and her daughter, Isabel Briggs Myers. They began creating the indicator during World War II, believing that a knowledge of personality preferences would help women who were entering the industrial workforce for the first time identify the sort of war-time jobs where they would be 'most comfortable and effective'.[xiii] The initial questionnaire grew into the _____, which was first published in 1962.
    a. 1990 Clean Air Act
    b. 33 Strategies of War
    c. 28-hour day
    d. Myers-Briggs Type Indicator

2. The _____ captures an expanded spectrum of values and criteria for measuring organizational success: economic, ecological and social. With the ratification of the United Nations and ICLEI _____ standard for urban and community accounting in early 2007, this became the dominant approach to public sector full cost accounting. Similar UN standards apply to natural capital and human capital measurement to assist in measurements required by _____, e.g. the ecoBudget standard for reporting ecological footprint.
    a. Triple bottom line
    b. 28-hour day
    c. 33 Strategies of War
    d. 1990 Clean Air Act

3. _____ generally refers to a list of all planned expenses and revenues. It is a plan for saving and spending. A _____ is an important concept in microeconomics, which uses a _____ line to illustrate the trade-offs between two or more goods.
    a. 1990 Clean Air Act
    b. 33 Strategies of War
    c. Budget
    d. 28-hour day

Chapter 4. Preparation and Alternatives

4. _____ refers to the movement of cash into or out of a business or financial product. It is usually measured during a specified, finite period of time. Measurement of _____ can be used

- to determine a project's rate of return or value. The time of _____s into and out of projects are used as inputs in financial models such as internal rate of return, and net present value.
- to determine problems with a business's liquidity. Being profitable does not necessarily mean being liquid. A company can fail because of a shortage of cash, even while profitable.
- as an alternate measure of a business's profits when it is believed that accrual accounting concepts do not represent economic realities. For example, a company may be notionally profitable but generating little operational cash (as may be the case for a company that barters its products rather than selling for cash.) In such a case, the company may be deriving additional operating cash by issuing shares evaluating default risk, re-investment requirements, etc.

_____ is a generic term used differently depending on the context. It may be defined by users for their own purposes.

 a. Cash flow
 b. Gross profit margin
 c. Sweat equity
 d. Gross profit

5. A _____ is a process in which a potential employee is evaluated by an employer for prospective employment in their company, organization and was established in the late 16th century.

A _____ typically precedes the hiring decision, and is used to evaluate the candidate. The interview is usually preceded by the evaluation of submitted résumés from interested candidates, then selecting a small number of candidates for interviews.

 a. Payrolling
 b. Supported employment
 c. Split shift
 d. Job interview

6. An _____, or organogram(me)) is a diagram that shows the structure of an organization and the relationships and relative ranks of its parts and positions/jobs. The term is also used for similar diagrams, for example ones showing the different elements of a field of knowledge or a group of languages. The French Encyclopédie had one of the first _____s of knowledge in general.
 a. AAAI
 b. Organizational chart
 c. A Stake in the Outcome
 d. A4e

Chapter 4. Preparation and Alternatives

7. A _____ is one scenario provided for evaluation by respondents in a Choice Experiment. Responses are collected and used to create a Choice Model. Respondents are usually provided with a series of differing _____s for evaluation.
   a. Choice Set
   b. Pairwise comparison
   c. Thurstone scale
   d. Computerized classification test

8. The process of _____ involves the introduction of a good or service that is new or substantially improved. This includes, but is not limited to, improvements in functional characteristics, technical abilities, or ease of use.
   a. Job enlargement
   b. Service-profit chain
   c. Letter of resignation
   d. Product innovation

9. _____ is a term developed by Eric von Hippel in 1986. His definition for _____ is:

   1. _____s face needs that will be general in a marketplace - but face them months or years before the bulk of that marketplace encounters them, and
   2. _____s are positioned to benefit significantly by obtaining a solution to those needs.

   In other words: _____s are users of a product that currently experience needs still unknown to the public and who also benefit greatly if they obtain a solution to these needs.

   The _____ Method is a market research tool that may be used by companies and / or individuals seeking to develop breakthrough products. _____ methodology was originally developed by Dr. Eric von Hippel of the Massachusetts Institute of Technology (MIT) and first described in the July 1986 issue of the Journal of Management Science.

   a. 1990 Clean Air Act
   b. Lead user
   c. 33 Strategies of War
   d. 28-hour day

10. In game theory, an _____ is a set of moves or strategies taken by the players, or their payoffs resulting from the actions or strategies taken by all players. The two are complementary in that given knowledge of the set of strategies of all players, the final state of the game is known, as are any relevant payoffs. In a game where chance or a random event is involved, the _____ is not known from only the set of strategies, but is only realized when the random event(s) are realized.

a. A Stake in the Outcome
b. A4e
c. AAAI
d. Outcome

11. _____ is a term promoted by Henry Chesbrough, a professor and executive director at the Center for _____ at Berkeley, in his book _____: The new imperative for creating and profiting from technology. The concept is related to user innovation, cumulative innovation and distributed innovation.

'_____ is a paradigm that assumes that firms can and should use external ideas as well as internal ideas, and internal and external paths to market, as the firms look to advance their technology'.

a. A Stake in the Outcome
b. A4e
c. Open innovation
d. AAAI

12. _____ is a term used to describe persistent social, corporate or institutional culture that avoids using or buying already existing products, research or knowledge because of its different origins. It is normally used in a pejorative sense.

As a social phenomenon, '_____' syndrome is manifested as an unwillingness to adopt an idea or product because it originates from another culture, a form of nationalism.

a. 33 Strategies of War
b. 28-hour day
c. 1990 Clean Air Act
d. Not invented here

13. Procter is a surname, and may also refer to:

- Bryan Waller Procter (pseud. Barry Cornwall), English poet
- Goodwin Procter, American law firm
- _____, consumer products multinational

a. Strict liability
b. Master and Servant Acts
c. Downstream
d. Procter ' Gamble

14. 'Speaking generally, properties are those physical quantities which directly describe the physical attributes of the system; _____s are those combinations of the properties which suffice to determine the response of the system. Properties can have all sorts of dimensions, depending upon the system being considered; _____s are dimensionless, or have the dimension of time or its reciprocal.'

The term can also be used in engineering contexts, however, as it is typically used in the physical sciences.

When the terms formal _____ and actual _____ are used, they generally correspond with the definitions used in computer science.

a. Parameter
b. 33 Strategies of War
c. 1990 Clean Air Act
d. 28-hour day

Chapter 5. Problem-Based Ideation: Finding and Solving Customers' Problems

1. _____ is an integrated communications-based process through which individuals and communities discover that existing and newly-identified needs and wants may be satisfied by the products and services of others.

_____ is defined by the American _____ Association as the activity, set of institutions, and processes for creating, communicating, delivering, and exchanging offerings that have value for customers, clients, partners, and society at large. The term developed from the original meaning which referred literally to going to market, as in shopping, or going to a market to buy or sell goods or services.

   a. Customer relationship management
   b. Disruptive technology
   c. Market development
   d. Marketing

2. In physics, and more specifically kinematics, _____ is the change in velocity over time. Because velocity is a vector, it can change in two ways: a change in magnitude and/or a change in direction. In one dimension, _____ is the rate at which something speeds up or slows down.

   a. A4e
   b. AAAI
   c. A Stake in the Outcome
   d. Acceleration

3. _____ is a group creativity technique designed to generate a large number of ideas for the solution of a problem. The method was first popularized in the late 1930s by Alex Faickney Osborn in a book called Applied Imagination. Osborn proposed that groups could double their creative output with _____.

   a. Affiliation
   b. Adam Smith
   c. Abraham Harold Maslow
   d. Brainstorming

4. In economics, _____ is a measure of the relative satisfaction from consumption of various goods and services. Given this measure, one may speak meaningfully of increasing or decreasing _____, and thereby explain economic behavior in terms of attempts to increase one's _____. For illustrative purposes, changes in _____ are sometimes expressed in units called utils.

   a. Utility
   b. A Stake in the Outcome
   c. Indirect utility function
   d. Ordinal utility

Chapter 5. Problem-Based Ideation: Finding and Solving Customers' Problems

5. _____ is a broad label that refers to any individuals or households that use goods and services generated within the economy. The concept of a _____ is used in different contexts, so that the usage and significance of the term may vary.

Typically when business people and economists talk of _____s they are talking about person as _____, an aggregated commodity item with little individuality other than that expressed in the buy/not-buy decision.

   a. 1990 Clean Air Act
   b. 33 Strategies of War
   c. 28-hour day
   d. Consumer

6. A _____ is a form of qualitative research in which a group of people are asked about their attitude towards a product, service, concept, advertisement, idea, or packaging. Questions are asked in an interactive group setting where participants are free to talk with other group members.

The first _____s were created at the Bureau of Applied Social Research by associate director, sociologist Robert K. Merton.

   a. Marketing research
   b. 1990 Clean Air Act
   c. Market analysis
   d. Focus group

7. _____ is a term developed by Eric von Hippel in 1986. His definition for _____ is:

   1. _____s face needs that will be general in a marketplace - but face them months or years before the bulk of that marketplace encounters them, and
   2. _____s are positioned to benefit significantly by obtaining a solution to those needs.

In other words: _____s are users of a product that currently experience needs still unknown to the public and who also benefit greatly if they obtain a solution to these needs.

The _____ Method is a market research tool that may be used by companies and / or individuals seeking to develop breakthrough products. _____ methodology was originally developed by Dr. Eric von Hippel of the Massachusetts Institute of Technology (MIT) and first described in the July 1986 issue of the Journal of Management Science.

Chapter 5. Problem-Based Ideation: Finding and Solving Customers' Problems

a. 1990 Clean Air Act
b. 28-hour day
c. 33 Strategies of War
d. Lead user

8. _____ is a term used in business and Information Technology (through ITIL) to describe the process of capturing a customer's requirements. Specifically, the _____ is a market research technique that produces a detailed set of customer wants and needs, organized into a hierarchical structure, and then prioritized in terms of relative importance and satisfaction with current alternatives. _____ studies typically consist of both qualitative and quantitative research steps.

a. Business philosophy
b. Goal setting
c. Board of governors
d. Voice of the customer

9. _____ is a strategic planning method that some organizations use to make flexible long-term plans. It is in large part an adaptation and generalization of classic methods used by military intelligence.

The original method was that a group of analysts would generate simulation games for policy makers. In business applications, the emphasis on gaming the behavior of opponents was reduced (shifting more toward a game against nature). At Royal Dutch/Shell for example, _____ was viewed as changing mindsets about the exogenous part of the world, prior to formulating specific strategies.

a. Labour productivity
b. Scenario planning
c. Time and attendance
d. Retroactive overtime

1. In marketing, _____ has come to mean the process by which marketers try to create an image or identity in the minds of their target market for its product, brand, or organization. It is the 'relative competitive comparison' their product occupies in a given market as perceived by the target market.

Re-_____ involves changing the identity of a product, relative to the identity of competing products, in the collective minds of the target market.

   a. Customer analytics
   b. PEST analysis
   c. Context analysis
   d. Positioning

2. In business and economics, _____ is a business resource assessment tool enabling a company to compare its actual performance with its potential performance. At its core are two questions: 'Where are we?' and 'Where do we want to be?' If a company or organization is under-utilizing its current resources or is forgoing investment in capital or technology, then it may be producing or performing at a level below its potential. This concept is similar to the base case of being below one's production possibilities frontier.
   a. Cross-selling
   b. Gap analysis
   c. Yield management
   d. Business networking

3. _____ or clustering is the assignment of a set of observations into subsets (called clusters) so that observations in the same cluster are similar in some sense. Clustering is a method of unsupervised learning, and a common technique for statistical data analysis used in many fields, including machine learning, data mining, pattern recognition, image analysis and bioinformatics.

Besides the term clustering, there are a number of terms with similar meanings, including automatic classification, numerical taxonomy, botryology and typological analysis.

   a. Cluster analysis
   b. 28-hour day
   c. Decision tree learning
   d. 1990 Clean Air Act

4. _____ is a statistical method used to describe variability among observed variables in terms of fewer unobserved variables called factors. The observed variables are modeled as linear combinations of the factors, plus 'error' terms. The information gained about the interdependencies can be used later to reduce the set of variables in a dataset.

Chapter 6. Analytical Attribute Approaches: Introduction and Perceptual Mapping

a. Rating scale
b. Computer-adaptive testing
c. Factor analysis
d. Multistage testing

5. A _____ is a research instrument consisting of a series of questions and other prompts for the purpose of gathering information from respondents. Although they are often designed for statistical analysis of the responses, this is not always the case. The _____ was invented by Sir Francis Galton.
   a. Questionnaire construction
   b. Structured interview
   c. Questionnaire
   d. Mystery shoppers

6. _____-model (SCOR(r)) is a process reference model developed by the management consulting firm PRTM and AMR Research and endorsed by the Supply-Chain Council (SCC) as the cross-industry de facto standard diagnostic tool for supply chain management. SCOR enables users to address, improve, and communicate supply chain management practices within and between all interested parties in the Extended Enterprise.

    SCOR(r) is a management tool, spanning from the supplier's supplier to the customer's customer. The model has been developed by the members of the Council on a volunteer basis to describe the business activities associated with all phases of satisfying a customer's demand.

   a. Supply chain management software
   b. Supply Chain Risk Management
   c. Supply-Chain Operations Reference
   d. Delayed differentiation

7. _____ is a set of related statistical techniques often used in information visualization for exploring similarities or dissimilarities in data. MDS is a special case of ordination. An MDS algorithm starts with a matrix of item-item similarities, then assigns a location to each item in N-dimensional space, where N is specified a priori.
   a. 1990 Clean Air Act
   b. 28-hour day
   c. Convenience
   d. Multidimensional scaling

8. _____ is a graphics technique used by asset marketers that attempts to visually display the perceptions of customers or potential customers. Typically the position of a product, product line, brand, or company is displayed relative to their competition.

Perceptual maps can have any number of dimensions but the most common is two dimensions.

a. Perceptual mapping
b. Product differentiation
c. PEST analysis
d. Mass marketing

Chapter 7. Analytical Attribute Approaches: Trade-off Analysis and Qualitative Techniques

1. _____ is a statistical technique that originated in mathematical psychology. Today it is used in many of the social sciences and applied sciences including marketing, product management, and operations research. It is not to be confused with the theory of conjoint measurement.
   a. Conjoint analysis
   b. Classical test theory
   c. Semantic differential
   d. Counternull

2. The process of _____ involves the introduction of a good or service that is new or substantially improved. This includes, but is not limited to, improvements in functional characteristics, technical abilities, or ease of use.
   a. Job enlargement
   b. Product innovation
   c. Service-profit chain
   d. Letter of resignation

3. _____ is an advertisement in which a particular product specifically mentions a competitor by name for the express purpose of showing why the competitor is inferior to the product naming it.

This should not be confused with parody advertisements, where a fictional product is being advertised for the purpose of poking fun at the particular advertisement, nor should it be confused with the use of a coined brand name for the purpose of comparing the product without actually naming an actual competitor. ('Wikipedia tastes better and is less filling than the Encyclopedia Galactica.')

In the 1980s, during what has been referred to as the cola wars, soft-drink manufacturer Pepsi ran a series of advertisements where people, caught on hidden camera, in a blind taste test, chose Pepsi over rival Coca-Cola.

   a. Comparative advertising
   b. 1990 Clean Air Act
   c. 33 Strategies of War
   d. 28-hour day

4. A _____ is a set of consistent ethic values (more specifically the personal and cultural values) and measures used for the purpose of ethical or ideological integrity. A well defined _____ is a moral code.

Chapter 7. Analytical Attribute Approaches: Trade-off Analysis and Qualitative Techniques

Fred Wenst>øp and Arild Myrmel have proposed a structure for corporate _____s that consists of three value categories. These are considered complementary and juxtaposed on the same level if illustrated graphically on for instance an organization's web page. The first value category is Core Values, which prescribe the attitude and character of an organization, and are often found in sections on Code of conduct on its web page. The philosophical antecedents of these values are Virtue ethics, which is often attributed to Aristotle. Protected Values are protected through rules, standards and certifications. They are often concerned with areas such as health, environment and safety. The third category, Created Values, is the values that stakeholders, including the shareholders expect in return for their contributions to the firm. These values are subject to trade-off by decision-makers or bargaining processes. This process is explained further in Stakeholder theory.

a. 28-hour day
b. 1990 Clean Air Act
c. Value system
d. 33 Strategies of War

5. _____ is the corporate management term for the act of reorganizing the legal, ownership, operational, or other structures of a company for the purpose of making it more profitable, or better organized for its present needs. Alternate reasons for _____ include a change of ownership or ownership structure, demerger repositioning debt _____ and financial _____.
   a. Market value
   b. Restructuring
   c. Net worth
   d. Market value added

6. In physics, and more specifically kinematics, _____ is the change in velocity over time. Because velocity is a vector, it can change in two ways: a change in magnitude and/or a change in direction. In one dimension, _____ is the rate at which something speeds up or slows down.
   a. AAAI
   b. A4e
   c. Acceleration
   d. A Stake in the Outcome

7. _____ is one of the managerial functions like planning, organizing, staffing and directing. It is an important function because it helps to check the errors and to take the corrective action so that deviation from standards are minimized and stated goals of the organization are achieved in desired manner.According to modern concepts, _____ is a foreseeing action whereas earlier concept of _____ was used only when errors were detected. _____ in management means setting standards, measuring actual performance and taking corrective action.

a. Control
b. Schedule of reinforcement
c. Turnover
d. Decision tree pruning

8. In economics, _____ is a measure of the relative satisfaction from consumption of various goods and services. Given this measure, one may speak meaningfully of increasing or decreasing _____, and thereby explain economic behavior in terms of attempts to increase one's _____. For illustrative purposes, changes in _____ are sometimes expressed in units called utils.

   a. Indirect utility function
   b. A Stake in the Outcome
   c. Ordinal utility
   d. Utility

9. _____ is a strategic planning method that some organizations use to make flexible long-term plans. It is in large part an adaptation and generalization of classic methods used by military intelligence.

The original method was that a group of analysts would generate simulation games for policy makers. In business applications, the emphasis on gaming the behavior of opponents was reduced (shifting more toward a game against nature). At Royal Dutch/Shell for example, _____ was viewed as changing mindsets about the exogenous part of the world, prior to formulating specific strategies.

   a. Labour productivity
   b. Time and attendance
   c. Scenario planning
   d. Retroactive overtime

Chapter 8. The Concept Evaluation System

1. There are many important decisions about product and service development and marketing. In the process of product development and marketing we should focus on strategic decisions about product attributes, product branding, product packaging, product labeling and product support services. But product strategy also calls for building a _____.
   a. Context analysis
   b. Product bundling
   c. Marketing strategy
   d. Product line

2. _____ refers to the movement of cash into or out of a business or financial product. It is usually measured during a specified, finite period of time. Measurement of _____ can be used

   - to determine a project's rate of return or value. The time of _____s into and out of projects are used as inputs in financial models such as internal rate of return, and net present value.
   - to determine problems with a business's liquidity. Being profitable does not necessarily mean being liquid. A company can fail because of a shortage of cash, even while profitable.
   - as an alternate measure of a business's profits when it is believed that accrual accounting concepts do not represent economic realities. For example, a company may be notionally profitable but generating little operational cash (as may be the case for a company that barters its products rather than selling for cash.) In such a case, the company may be deriving additional operating cash by issuing shares evaluating default risk, re-investment requirements, etc.

   _____ is a generic term used differently depending on the context. It may be defined by users for their own purposes.

   a. Gross profit margin
   b. Sweat equity
   c. Gross profit
   d. Cash flow

3. _____ or economic opportunity loss is the value of the next best alternative forgone as the result of making a decision. _____ analysis is an important part of a company's decision-making processes but is not treated as an actual cost in any financial statement. The next best thing that a person can engage in is referred to as the _____ of doing the best thing and ignoring the next best thing to be done.
   a. Opportunity cost
   b. AAAI
   c. A4e
   d. A Stake in the Outcome

4. In economics, business, retail, and accounting, a _____ is the value of money that has been used up to produce something, and hence is not available for use anymore. In economics, a _____ is an alternative that is given up as a result of a decision. In business, the _____ may be one of acquisition, in which case the amount of money expended to acquire it is counted as _____.

a. Fixed costs
b. Cost overrun
c. Cost allocation
d. Cost

5. In decision theory and estimation theory, the _____ of an estimator, $\hat{\theta}$, of an unknown parameter of the distribution, θ, is the expected value of the loss function

$$R(\theta, \hat{\theta}) = \mathbb{E}_\theta L(\theta, \hat{\theta}) = \int L(\theta, \hat{\theta})\, dP_\theta.$$

where dP_θ is a probability measure parametrized by θ.

- For a scalar parameter θ and a quadratic loss function,

$$L(\theta, \hat{\theta}) = (\theta - \hat{\theta})^2$$

  the _____ function becomes the mean squared error of the estimate,

$$R(\theta, \hat{\theta}) = E_\theta(\theta - \hat{\theta})^2$$

- In density estimation, the unknown parameter is probability density itself. The loss function is typically chosen to be a norm in an appropriate function space. For example, for L^2 norm,

$$L(f, \hat{f}) = \|f - \hat{f}\|_2^2$$

  the _____ function becomes the mean integrated squared error

$$R(f, \hat{f}) = E\|f - \hat{f}\|^2$$

a. Risk
b. Financial modeling
c. Linear model
d. Risk aversion

6. _____ refers to an assessment of the viability, stability and profitability of a business, sub-business or project.

It is performed by professionals who prepare reports using ratios that make use of information taken from financial statements and other reports. These reports are usually presented to top management as one of their bases in making business decisions.

   a. 33 Strategies of War
   b. 28-hour day
   c. Financial analysis
   d. 1990 Clean Air Act

7. _____ is an integrated communications-based process through which individuals and communities discover that existing and newly-identified needs and wants may be satisfied by the products and services of others.

_____ is defined by the American _____ Association as the activity, set of institutions, and processes for creating, communicating, delivering, and exchanging offerings that have value for customers, clients, partners, and society at large. The term developed from the original meaning which referred literally to going to market, as in shopping, or going to a market to buy or sell goods or services.

   a. Disruptive technology
   b. Customer relationship management
   c. Market development
   d. Marketing

8. The process of _____ involves the introduction of a good or service that is new or substantially improved. This includes, but is not limited to, improvements in functional characteristics, technical abilities, or ease of use.
   a. Job enlargement
   b. Service-profit chain
   c. Letter of resignation
   d. Product innovation

9. The _____ captures an expanded spectrum of values and criteria for measuring organizational success: economic, ecological and social. With the ratification of the United Nations and ICLEI _____ standard for urban and community accounting in early 2007, this became the dominant approach to public sector full cost accounting. Similar UN standards apply to natural capital and human capital measurement to assist in measurements required by _____, e.g. the ecoBudget standard for reporting ecological footprint.

a. 1990 Clean Air Act
b. 33 Strategies of War
c. 28-hour day
d. Triple bottom line

10. In business and engineering, new _____ is the term used to describe the complete process of bringing a new product or service to market. There are two parallel paths involved in the NProduct development process: one involves the idea generation, product design, and detail engineering; the other involves market research and marketing analysis. Companies typically see new _____ as the first stage in generating and commercializing new products within the overall strategic process of product life cycle management used to maintain or grow their market share.
   a. Product development
   b. 28-hour day
   c. 1990 Clean Air Act
   d. 33 Strategies of War

11. _____ is the process by which a new idea or new product is accepted by the market. The rate of _____ is the speed that the new idea spreads from one consumer to the next. Adoption is similar to _____ except that it deals with the psychological processes an individual goes through, rather than an aggregate market process.
   a. Mass marketing
   b. Category management
   c. Value chain
   d. Diffusion

12. _____ is the process of estimation in unknown situations. Prediction is a similar, but more general term. Both can refer to estimation of time series, cross-sectional or longitudinal data.
   a. 28-hour day
   b. 33 Strategies of War
   c. Forecasting
   d. 1990 Clean Air Act

13. _____ is a broad label that refers to any individuals or households that use goods and services generated within the economy. The concept of a _____ is used in different contexts, so that the usage and significance of the term may vary.

Typically when business people and economists talk of _____s they are talking about person as _____, an aggregated commodity item with little individuality other than that expressed in the buy/not-buy decision.

a. 33 Strategies of War
b. 28-hour day
c. Consumer
d. 1990 Clean Air Act

Chapter 9. Concept Testing

1. In marketing, _____ has come to mean the process by which marketers try to create an image or identity in the minds of their target market for its product, brand, or organization. It is the 'relative competitive comparison' their product occupies in a given market as perceived by the target market.

   Re-_____ involves changing the identity of a product, relative to the identity of competing products, in the collective minds of the target market.

   a. Positioning
   b. PEST analysis
   c. Customer analytics
   d. Context analysis

2. A _____ is a documented investigation of a Market that is used to inform a firm's planning activities particularly around decision of: inventory, purchase, work force expansion/contraction, facility expansion, purchases of capital equipment, promotional activities, and many other aspects of a company.

   Not all managers are asked to conduct a _____, but all managers must make decisions using _____ data and understand how the data was derived. So all managers need a reasonable understanding of the tools most used for making sales forecasts and analyzing markets.

   a. Marketing research process
   b. 1990 Clean Air Act
   c. Marketing research
   d. Market analysis

3. A _____ is a process in which a potential employee is evaluated by an employer for prospective employment in their company, organization and was established in the late 16th century.

   A _____ typically precedes the hiring decision, and is used to evaluate the candidate. The interview is usually preceded by the evaluation of submitted résumés from interested candidates, then selecting a small number of candidates for interviews.

   a. Job interview
   b. Split shift
   c. Payrolling
   d. Supported employment

4. _____ is an adjective for experience-based techniques that help in problem solving, learning and discovery. A _____ method is particularly used to rapidly come to a solution that is hoped to be close to the best possible answer, or 'optimal solution'. _____s are 'rules of thumb', educated guesses, intuitive judgments or simply common sense.

Chapter 9. Concept Testing

a. 28-hour day
b. 1990 Clean Air Act
c. Representativeness
d. Heuristic

5. _____, in strategic management and marketing is, according to Carlton O'Neal, the percentage or proportion of the total available market or market segment that is being serviced by a company. It can be expressed as a company's sales revenue (from that market) divided by the total sales revenue available in that market. It can also be expressed as a company's unit sales volume (in a market) divided by the total volume of units sold in that market.

a. Market share
b. Marketing plan
c. Business-to-business
d. Green marketing

6. _____-model (SCOR(r)) is a process reference model developed by the management consulting firm PRTM and AMR Research and endorsed by the Supply-Chain Council (SCC) as the cross-industry de facto standard diagnostic tool for supply chain management. SCOR enables users to address, improve, and communicate supply chain management practices within and between all interested parties in the Extended Enterprise.

SCOR(r) is a management tool, spanning from the supplier's supplier to the customer's customer. The model has been developed by the members of the Council on a volunteer basis to describe the business activities associated with all phases of satisfying a customer's demand.

a. Delayed differentiation
b. Supply Chain Risk Management
c. Supply chain management software
d. Supply-Chain Operations Reference

7. _____ of the learning curve effect and the closely related experience curve effect express the relationship between equations for experience and efficiency or between efficiency gains and investment in the effort. The experience of 'learning curves' was first observed by the 19th Century German psychologist Hermann Ebbinghaus according to the difficulty of memorizing varying numbers of verbal stimuli, and subsequent learning about the complex processes of learning are discussed in the

The rule used for representing the learning curve effect states that the more times a task has been performed, the less time will be required on each subsequent iteration.

Chapter 9. Concept Testing

a. Spatial Decision Support Systems
b. Distribution
c. Point biserial correlation coefficient
d. Models

8. _____ is one of the four Ps of the marketing mix. The other three aspects are product, promotion, and place. It is also a key variable in microeconomic price allocation theory.
   a. Pricing
   b. Transfer pricing
   c. Price floor
   d. Penetration pricing

9. _____ is a group creativity technique designed to generate a large number of ideas for the solution of a problem. The method was first popularized in the late 1930s by Alex Faickney Osborn in a book called Applied Imagination. Osborn proposed that groups could double their creative output with _____.
   a. Adam Smith
   b. Affiliation
   c. Abraham Harold Maslow
   d. Brainstorming

10. _____ or clustering is the assignment of a set of observations into subsets (called clusters) so that observations in the same cluster are similar in some sense. Clustering is a method of unsupervised learning, and a common technique for statistical data analysis used in many fields, including machine learning, data mining, pattern recognition, image analysis and bioinformatics.

Besides the term clustering, there are a number of terms with similar meanings, including automatic classification, numerical taxonomy, botryology and typological analysis.

   a. Decision tree learning
   b. Cluster analysis
   c. 28-hour day
   d. 1990 Clean Air Act

11. A _____ is a name or trademark connected with a product or producer. _____s have become increasingly important components of culture and the economy, now being described as 'cultural accessories and personal philosophies'.

Some people distinguish the psychological aspect of a _____ from the experiential aspect.

a. Brand
b. Brand loyalty
c. Brand extension
d. Brand awareness

12. _____ is a statistical technique that originated in mathematical psychology. Today it is used in many of the social sciences and applied sciences including marketing, product management, and operations research. It is not to be confused with the theory of conjoint measurement.
a. Semantic differential
b. Classical test theory
c. Counternull
d. Conjoint analysis

Chapter 10. The Full Screen

1. _____ of the learning curve effect and the closely related experience curve effect express the relationship between equations for experience and efficiency or between efficiency gains and investment in the effort. The experience of 'learning curves' was first observed by the 19th Century German psychologist Hermann Ebbinghaus according to the difficulty of memorizing varying numbers of verbal stimuli, and subsequent learning about the complex processes of learning are discussed in the

.

The rule used for representing the learning curve effect states that the more times a task has been performed, the less time will be required on each subsequent iteration.

   a. Spatial Decision Support Systems
   b. Models
   c. Distribution
   d. Point biserial correlation coefficient

2. _____ or net present worth (NPW) is defined as the total present value (PV) of a time series of cash flows. It is a standard method for using the time value of money to appraise long-term projects. Used for capital budgeting, and widely throughout economics, it measures the excess or shortfall of cash flows, in present value terms, once financing charges are met.
   a. Present value
   b. 1990 Clean Air Act
   c. Net present value
   d. Discounted cash flow

3. _____ is the value on a given date of a future payment or series of future payments, discounted to reflect the time value of money and other factors such as investment risk. _____ calculations are widely used in business and economics to provide a means to compare cash flows at different times on a meaningful 'like to like' basis.

If offered a choice between $100 today or $100 in one year, everyone will choose $100 today.

   a. 1990 Clean Air Act
   b. Discounted cash flow
   c. Net present value
   d. Present value

4. A _____ is a name or trademark connected with a product or producer. _____s have become increasingly important components of culture and the economy, now being described as 'cultural accessories and personal philosophies'.

Some people distinguish the psychological aspect of a _____ from the experiential aspect.

a. Brand loyalty
b. Brand awareness
c. Brand extension
d. Brand

5. The _____ is a structured technique for dealing with complex decisions. Rather than prescribing a 'correct' decision, the _____ helps the decision makers find the one that best suits their needs and their understanding of the problem.

Based on mathematics and psychology, it was developed by Thomas L. Saaty in the 1970s and has been extensively studied and refined since then.

a. A4e
b. AAAI
c. Analytic Hierarchy Process
d. A Stake in the Outcome

6. _____ refers to the movement of cash into or out of a business or financial product. It is usually measured during a specified, finite period of time. Measurement of _____ can be used

- to determine a project's rate of return or value. The time of _____s into and out of projects are used as inputs in financial models such as internal rate of return, and net present value.
- to determine problems with a business's liquidity. Being profitable does not necessarily mean being liquid. A company can fail because of a shortage of cash, even while profitable.
- as an alternate measure of a business's profits when it is believed that accrual accounting concepts do not represent economic realities. For example, a company may be notionally profitable but generating little operational cash (as may be the case for a company that barters its products rather than selling for cash.) In such a case, the company may be deriving additional operating cash by issuing shares evaluating default risk, re-investment requirements, etc.

_____ is a generic term used differently depending on the context. It may be defined by users for their own purposes.

a. Cash flow
b. Sweat equity
c. Gross profit
d. Gross profit margin

7. A _____ is a decision support tool that uses a tree-like graph or model of decisions and their possible consequences, including chance event outcomes, resource costs, and utility. _____s are commonly used in operations research, specifically in decision analysis, to help identify a strategy most likely to reach a goal. Another use of _____s is as a descriptive means for calculating conditional probabilities.
   a. 33 Strategies of War
   b. 28-hour day
   c. 1990 Clean Air Act
   d. Decision tree

8. An _____ is software that attempts to reproduce the performance of one or more human experts, most commonly in a specific problem domain, and is a traditional application and/or subfield of artificial intelligence. A wide variety of methods can be used to simulate the performance of the expert however common to most or all are 1) the creation of a so-called 'knowledgebase' which uses some knowledge representation formalism to capture the Subject Matter Experts (SME) knowledge and 2) a process of gathering that knowledge from the SME and codifying it according to the formalism, which is called knowledge engineering. _____s may or may not have learning components but a third common element is that once the system is developed it is proven by being placed in the same real world problem solving situation as the human SME, typically as an aid to human workers or a supplement to some information system.
   a. AAAI
   b. A4e
   c. A Stake in the Outcome
   d. Expert system

Chapter 11. Sales Forecasting and Financial Analysis

1. _____ is the process of estimation in unknown situations. Prediction is a similar, but more general term. Both can refer to estimation of time series, cross-sectional or longitudinal data.
   a. 1990 Clean Air Act
   b. 28-hour day
   c. 33 Strategies of War
   d. Forecasting

2. _____ of the learning curve effect and the closely related experience curve effect express the relationship between equations for experience and efficiency or between efficiency gains and investment in the effort. The experience of 'learning curves' was first observed by the 19th Century German psychologist Hermann Ebbinghaus according to the difficulty of memorizing varying numbers of verbal stimuli, and subsequent learning about the complex processes of learning are discussed in the

   .

   The rule used for representing the learning curve effect states that the more times a task has been performed, the less time will be required on each subsequent iteration.

   a. Spatial Decision Support Systems
   b. Distribution
   c. Point biserial correlation coefficient
   d. Models

3. In statistics, signal processing, and many other fields, a _____ is a sequence of data points, measured typically at successive times, spaced at (often uniform) time intervals. _____ analysis comprises methods that attempt to understand such _____, often either to understand the underlying context of the data points (Where did they come from? What generated them?), or to make forecasts (predictions.) _____ forecasting is the use of a model to forecast future events based on known past events: to forecast future data points before they are measured.
   a. Histogram
   b. Standard deviation
   c. Moving average
   d. Time series

4. _____, in strategic management and marketing is, according to Carlton O'Neal, the percentage or proportion of the total available market or market segment that is being serviced by a company. It can be expressed as a company's sales revenue (from that market) divided by the total sales revenue available in that market. It can also be expressed as a company's unit sales volume (in a market) divided by the total volume of units sold in that market.

Chapter 11. Sales Forecasting and Financial Analysis

a. Business-to-business
b. Green marketing
c. Marketing plan
d. Market share

5. _____ is the process by which a new idea or new product is accepted by the market. The rate of _____ is the speed that the new idea spreads from one consumer to the next. Adoption is similar to _____ except that it deals with the psychological processes an individual goes through, rather than an aggregate market process.

a. Mass marketing
b. Category management
c. Value chain
d. Diffusion

6. The process of _____ involves the introduction of a good or service that is new or substantially improved. This includes, but is not limited to, improvements in functional characteristics, technical abilities, or ease of use.

a. Service-profit chain
b. Letter of resignation
c. Job enlargement
d. Product innovation

7. _____ is one of the four Ps of the marketing mix. The other three aspects are product, promotion, and place. It is also a key variable in microeconomic price allocation theory.

a. Pricing
b. Price floor
c. Transfer pricing
d. Penetration pricing

8. _____ refers to an assessment of the viability, stability and profitability of a business, sub-business or project.

It is performed by professionals who prepare reports using ratios that make use of information taken from financial statements and other reports. These reports are usually presented to top management as one of their bases in making business decisions.

Chapter 11. Sales Forecasting and Financial Analysis

a. 28-hour day
b. 1990 Clean Air Act
c. 33 Strategies of War
d. Financial analysis

9. _____ refers to the movement of cash into or out of a business or financial product. It is usually measured during a specified, finite period of time. Measurement of _____ can be used

- to determine a project's rate of return or value. The time of _____s into and out of projects are used as inputs in financial models such as internal rate of return, and net present value.
- to determine problems with a business's liquidity. Being profitable does not necessarily mean being liquid. A company can fail because of a shortage of cash, even while profitable.
- as an alternate measure of a business's profits when it is believed that accrual accounting concepts do not represent economic realities. For example, a company may be notionally profitable but generating little operational cash (as may be the case for a company that barters its products rather than selling for cash.) In such a case, the company may be deriving additional operating cash by issuing shares evaluating default risk, re-investment requirements, etc.

_____ is a generic term used differently depending on the context. It may be defined by users for their own purposes.

a. Sweat equity
b. Gross profit margin
c. Gross profit
d. Cash flow

10. _____ has been described as the 'process of social influence in which one person can enlist the aid and support of others in the accomplishment of a common task' . A definition more inclusive of followers comes from Alan Keith of Genentech who said '_____ is ultimately about creating a way for people to contribute to making something extraordinary happen.'

_____ is one of the most salient aspects of the organizational context. However, defining _____ has been challenging.

a. 28-hour day
b. 1990 Clean Air Act
c. Situational leadership
d. Leadership

Chapter 11. Sales Forecasting and Financial Analysis

11. In decision theory and estimation theory, the _____ of an estimator, $\hat{\theta}$, of an unknown parameter of the distribution, θ, is the expected value of the loss function

$$R(\theta, \hat{\theta}) = \mathbb{E}_\theta L(\theta, \hat{\theta}) = \int L(\theta, \hat{\theta})\, dP_\theta.$$

where dP_θ is a probability measure parametrized by θ.

- For a scalar parameter θ and a quadratic loss function,

$$L(\theta, \hat{\theta}) = (\theta - \hat{\theta})^2$$

the _____ function becomes the mean squared error of the estimate,

$$R(\theta, \hat{\theta}) = E_\theta (\theta - \hat{\theta})^2$$

- In density estimation, the unknown parameter is probability density itself. The loss function is typically chosen to be a norm in an appropriate function space. For example, for L^2 norm,

$$L(f, \hat{f}) = \|f - \hat{f}\|_2^2$$

the _____ function becomes the mean integrated squared error

$$R(f, \hat{f}) = E \|f - \hat{f}\|^2$$

a. Linear model
b. Risk aversion
c. Financial modeling
d. Risk

12. In finance, _____, is the ratio of money gained or lost on an investment relative to the amount of money invested. The amount of money gained or lost may be referred to as interest, profit/loss, gain/loss, or net income/loss. The money invested may be referred to as the asset, capital, principal, or the cost basis of the investment.

a. Return on sales
b. Financial ratio
c. Return on Capital Employed
d. Rate of return

13. There are many important decisions about product and service development and marketing. In the process of product development and marketing we should focus on strategic decisions about product attributes, product branding, product packaging, product labeling and product support services. But product strategy also calls for building a _____.
   a. Context analysis
   b. Product line
   c. Product bundling
   d. Marketing strategy

14. The term _____ usually refers to a weighted arithmetic mean, but weighted versions of other means can also be calculated, such as the weighted geometric mean and the weighted harmonic mean.

Given two school classes, one with 20 students, and one with 30 students, the grades in each class on a test were:

   Morning class = 62, 67, 71, 74, 76, 77, 78, 79, 79, 80, 80, 81, 81, 82, 83, 84, 86, 89, 93, 98

   Afternoon class = 81, 82, 83, 84, 85, 86, 87, 87, 88, 88, 89, 89, 89, 90, 90, 90, 90, 91, 91, 91, 92, 92, 93, 93, 94, 95, 96, 97, 98, 99

The straight average for the morning class is 80 and the straight average of the afternoon class is 90. The straight average of 80 and 90 is 85, the mean of the two class means.

   a. 1990 Clean Air Act
   b. 33 Strategies of War
   c. 28-hour day
   d. Weighted average

15. The _____ is the rate (expressed as a percentage, like interest) that a company is expected to pay to debtholders (cost of debt) and shareholders (cost of equity) to finance its assets.

WACC is the minimum return that a company must earn on existing asset base to satisfy its creditors, owners, and other providers of capital. Companies raise money from a number of sources: common equity, preferred equity, straight debt, convertible debt, exchangeable debt, warrants, options, pension liabilities, executive stock options, governmental subsidies, and so on.

Chapter 11. Sales Forecasting and Financial Analysis

a. 1990 Clean Air Act
b. Capital intensive
c. Cost of capital
d. Weighted average cost of capital

16. In economics, business, retail, and accounting, a _____ is the value of money that has been used up to produce something, and hence is not available for use anymore. In economics, a _____ is an alternative that is given up as a result of a decision. In business, the _____ may be one of acquisition, in which case the amount of money expended to acquire it is counted as _____.

a. Cost overrun
b. Cost
c. Cost allocation
d. Fixed costs

17. The _____ is an expected return that the provider of capital plans to earn on their investment.

Capital (money) used for funding a business should earn returns for the capital providers who risk their capital. For an investment to be worthwhile, the expected return on capital must be greater than the _____.

a. Weighted average cost of capital
b. 1990 Clean Air Act
c. Capital intensive
d. Cost of capital

18. The _____ is an interest rate a central bank charges depository institutions that borrow reserves from it.

The term _____ has two meanings:

- the same as interest rate; the term 'discount' does not refer to the meaning of the word, but to the purpose of using the quantity, such as computations of present value, e.g. net present value or discounted cash flow

- the annual effective _____, which is the annual interest divided by the capital including that interest; this rate is lower than the interest rate; it corresponds to using the value after a year as the nominal value, and seeing the initial value as the nominal value minus a discount; it is used for Treasury Bills and similar financial instruments

The annual effective _____ is the annual interest divided by the capital including that interest, which is the interest rate divided by 100% plus the interest rate. It is the annual discount factor to be applied to the future cash flow, to find the discount, subtracted from a future value to find the value one year earlier.

For example, suppose there is a government bond that sells for $95 and pays $100 in a year's time.

   a. 33 Strategies of War
   b. Discount rate
   c. 28-hour day
   d. 1990 Clean Air Act

19. In economics and business decision-making, _____ are costs that cannot be recovered once they have been incurred. _____ are sometimes contrasted with variable costs, which are the costs that will change due to the proposed course of action, and prospective costs which are costs that will be incurred if an action is taken.

In traditional microeconomic theory, only variable costs are relevant to a decision.

   a. Pygmalion effect
   b. Cognitive biases
   c. Sunk costs
   d. Fundamental attribution error

Chapter 12. Product Protocol

1. In commerce, _____ is the length of time it takes from a product being conceived until its being available for sale. _____ is important in industries where products are outmoded quickly. A common assumption is that _____ matters most for first-of-a-kind products, but actually the leader often has the luxury of time, while the clock is clearly running for the followers.
    a. Career development
    b. Time to market
    c. Procurement
    d. Market entry

2. In physics, and more specifically kinematics, _____ is the change in velocity over time. Because velocity is a vector, it can change in two ways: a change in magnitude and/or a change in direction. In one dimension, _____ is the rate at which something speeds up or slows down.
    a. AAAI
    b. A Stake in the Outcome
    c. A4e
    d. Acceleration

3. In marketing, _____ has come to mean the process by which marketers try to create an image or identity in the minds of their target market for its product, brand, or organization. It is the 'relative competitive comparison' their product occupies in a given market as perceived by the target market.

    Re-_____ involves changing the identity of a product, relative to the identity of competing products, in the collective minds of the target market.

    a. Customer analytics
    b. Context analysis
    c. PEST analysis
    d. Positioning

4. _____ is an integrated communications-based process through which individuals and communities discover that existing and newly-identified needs and wants may be satisfied by the products and services of others.

    _____ is defined by the American _____ Association as the activity, set of institutions, and processes for creating, communicating, delivering, and exchanging offerings that have value for customers, clients, partners, and society at large. The term developed from the original meaning which referred literally to going to market, as in shopping, or going to a market to buy or sell goods or services.

a. Marketing
b. Market development
c. Customer relationship management
d. Disruptive technology

5. _____ refers to the overarching strategy of the diversified firm. Such a _____ answers the questions of 'in which businesses should we be in?' and 'how does being in these business create synergy and/or add to the competitive advantage of the corporation as a whole?'

Business strategy refers to the aggregated strategies of single business firm or a strategic business unit (SBU) in a diversified corporation. According to Michael Porter, a firm must formulate a business strategy that incorporates either cost leadership, differentiation or focus in order to achieve a sustainable competitive advantage and long-term success in its chosen arenas or industries.

a. Corporate strategy
b. Strategic drift
c. Competitive heterogeneity
d. Strategic group

6. _____ is a term used in business and Information Technology (through ITIL) to describe the process of capturing a customer's requirements. Specifically, the _____ is a market research technique that produces a detailed set of customer wants and needs, organized into a hierarchical structure, and then prioritized in terms of relative importance and satisfaction with current alternatives. _____ studies typically consist of both qualitative and quantitative research steps.

a. Goal setting
b. Business philosophy
c. Board of governors
d. Voice of the customer

7. A _____ is a process in which a potential employee is evaluated by an employer for prospective employment in their company, organization and was established in the late 16th century.

A _____ typically precedes the hiring decision, and is used to evaluate the candidate. The interview is usually preceded by the evaluation of submitted résumés from interested candidates, then selecting a small number of candidates for interviews.

Chapter 12. Product Protocol

a. Payrolling
b. Job interview
c. Split shift
d. Supported employment

8. _____ is the state or fact of exclusive rights and control over property, which may be an object, land/real estate or intellectual property. An _____ right is also referred to as title. The concept of _____ has existed for thousands of years and in all cultures.

a. A4e
b. A Stake in the Outcome
c. Emanation of the state
d. Ownership

9. The Program (or Project) Evaluation and Review Technique, commonly abbreviated _____, is a model for project management designed to analyze and represent the tasks involved in completing a given project.

_____ is a method to analyze the involved tasks in completing a given project, specially the time needed to complete each task, and identifying the minimum time needed to complete the total project.

_____ was developed primarily to simplify the planning and scheduling of large and complex projects.

a. 33 Strategies of War
b. 28-hour day
c. 1990 Clean Air Act
d. PERT

10. _____ is the process of estimation in unknown situations. Prediction is a similar, but more general term. Both can refer to estimation of time series, cross-sectional or longitudinal data.

a. 33 Strategies of War
b. 1990 Clean Air Act
c. 28-hour day
d. Forecasting

Chapter 13. Design

1. _____ is used for the design, development, analysis, and optimization of technical processes and is mainly applied to chemical plants and chemical processes, but also to power stations, and similar technical facilities. Process flow diagram of a typical amine treating process used in industrial plants

_____ is a model-based representation of chemical, physical, biological, and other technical processes and unit operations in software. Basic prerequisites are a thorough knowledge of chemical and physical properties of pure components and mixtures, of reactions, and of mathematical models which, in combination, allow the calculation of a process in computers.

   a. 1990 Clean Air Act
   b. Process simulation
   c. 28-hour day
   d. 33 Strategies of War

2. In economics, _____ is a measure of the relative satisfaction from consumption of various goods and services. Given this measure, one may speak meaningfully of increasing or decreasing _____, and thereby explain economic behavior in terms of attempts to increase one's _____. For illustrative purposes, changes in _____ are sometimes expressed in units called utils.

   a. Ordinal utility
   b. Indirect utility function
   c. A Stake in the Outcome
   d. Utility

3. _____ is a relatively new paradigm that emerged from 'barrier-free' or 'accessible design' and 'assistive technology.' _____ strives to be a broad-spectrum solution that produces buildings, products and environments that are usable and effective for everyone, not just people with disabilities. Moreover, it recognizes the importance of how things look. For example, while built up handles are a way to make utensils more usable for people with gripping limitations, some companies introduced larger, easy to grip and attractive handles as feature of mass produced utensils.

   a. AAAI
   b. A4e
   c. A Stake in the Outcome
   d. Universal design

4. _____s is the science of designing the job, equipment, and workplace to fit the worker. Proper _____ design is necessary to prevent repetitive strain injuries, which can develop over time and can lead to long-term disability.

_____s is concerned with the 'fit' between people and their work.

a. AAAI
b. Ergonomic
c. A Stake in the Outcome
d. A4e

5. _____ of the learning curve effect and the closely related experience curve effect express the relationship between equations for experience and efficiency or between efficiency gains and investment in the effort. The experience of 'learning curves' was first observed by the 19th Century German psychologist Hermann Ebbinghaus according to the difficulty of memorizing varying numbers of verbal stimuli, and subsequent learning about the complex processes of learning are discussed in the

.

The rule used for representing the learning curve effect states that the more times a task has been performed, the less time will be required on each subsequent iteration.

a. Spatial Decision Support Systems
b. Distribution
c. Point biserial correlation coefficient
d. Models

6. 'Speaking generally, properties are those physical quantities which directly describe the physical attributes of the system; _____s are those combinations of the properties which suffice to determine the response of the system. Properties can have all sorts of dimensions, depending upon the system being considered; _____s are dimensionless, or have the dimension of time or its reciprocal.'

The term can also be used in engineering contexts, however, as it is typically used in the physical sciences.

When the terms formal _____ and actual _____ are used, they generally correspond with the definitions used in computer science.

a. 33 Strategies of War
b. Parameter
c. 1990 Clean Air Act
d. 28-hour day

7. _____ can be defined as the idea generation, concept development, testing and manufacturing or implementation of a physical object or service. _____ers conceptualize and evaluate ideas, making them tangible through products in a more systematic approach. The role of a _____er encompasses many characteristics of the marketing manager, product manager, industrial designer and design engineer.

a. Abraham Harold Maslow
b. Adam Smith
c. Affiliation
d. Product design

8. _____ is the use of information technology to support engineers in tasks such as analysis, simulation, design, manufacture, planning, diagnosis, and repair.

Software tools that have been developed to support these activities are considered CAE tools. CAE tools are being used, for example, to analyze the robustness and performance of components and assemblies.

a. 1990 Clean Air Act
b. 33 Strategies of War
c. Computer-aided engineering
d. 28-hour day

9. _____ is the automatic construction of physical objects using solid freeform fabrication. The first techniques for _____ became available in the late 1980s and were used to produce models and prototype parts. Today, they are used for a much wider range of applications and are even used to manufacture production quality parts in relatively small numbers.

a. 1990 Clean Air Act
b. Rapid prototyping
c. 33 Strategies of War
d. 28-hour day

10. _____ is a term used in business and Information Technology (through ITIL) to describe the process of capturing a customer's requirements. Specifically, the _____ is a market research technique that produces a detailed set of customer wants and needs, organized into a hierarchical structure, and then prioritized in terms of relative importance and satisfaction with current alternatives. _____ studies typically consist of both qualitative and quantitative research steps.

a. Goal setting
b. Business philosophy
c. Voice of the customer
d. Board of governors

11. In probability theory, a probability distribution is called _____ if its cumulative distribution function is _____. This is equivalent to saying that for random variables X with the distribution in question, Pr[X = a] = 0 for all real numbers a, i.e.: the probability that X attains the value a is zero, for any number a. If the distribution of X is _____ then X is called a _____ random variable.

Chapter 13. Design

a. Decision tree pruning
b. Continuous
c. Connectionist expert systems
d. Pay Band

12. _____ is a management process whereby delivery (customer valued) processes are constantly evaluated and improved in the light of their efficiency, effectiveness and flexibility.

Some see it as a meta process for most management systems (Business Process Management, Quality Management, Project Management). Deming saw it as part of the 'system' whereby feedback from the process and customer were evaluated against organisational goals.

a. First-mover advantage
b. Sole proprietorship
c. Critical Success Factor
d. Continuous Improvement Process

13. The _____ Automobile Company is an automobile manufacturer based in Wolfsburg, Germany, and is the original brand within the _____ Group, as well as the largest brand by sales volume.

_____ means 'people's car' in German, in which it is pronounced . Its current tagline or slogan is Das Auto .

a. Rate of return
b. Turnover
c. Competence-based Strategic Management
d. Volkswagen

14. A _____ is a type of business entity in which partners (owners) share with each other the profits or losses of the business. _____s are often favored over corporations for taxation purposes, as the _____ structure does not generally incur a tax on profits before it is distributed to the partners (i.e. there is no dividend tax levied.) However, depending on the _____ structure and the jurisdiction in which it operates, owners of a _____ may be exposed to greater personal liability than they would as shareholders of a corporation.

a. Federal Employers Liability Act
b. Partnership
c. Due process
d. Mediation

Chapter 14. Development Team Management

1. _____ is the state or fact of exclusive rights and control over property, which may be an object, land/real estate or intellectual property. An _____ right is also referred to as title. The concept of _____ has existed for thousands of years and in all cultures.
   a. A4e
   b. Emanation of the state
   c. A Stake in the Outcome
   d. Ownership

2. An _____ is a mostly hierarchical concept of subordination of entities that collaborate and contribute to serve one common aim.

Organizations are a variant of clustered entities. The structure of an organization is usually set up in many a styles, dependent on their objectives and ambience.

   a. Informal organization
   b. Open shop
   c. Organizational development
   d. Organizational structure

3. In finance, an _____ is a contract between a buyer and a seller that gives the buyer the right--but not the obligation-- to buy or to sell a particular asset (the underlying asset) at a later day at an agreed price. In return for granting the _____, the seller collects a payment (the premium) from the buyer. A call _____ gives the buyer the right to buy the underlying asset; a put _____ gives the buyer of the _____ the right to sell the underlying asset.
   a. A4e
   b. A Stake in the Outcome
   c. AAAI
   d. Option

4. _____ refers to the movement of cash into or out of a business or financial product. It is usually measured during a specified, finite period of time. Measurement of _____ can be used

   - to determine a project's rate of return or value. The time of _____s into and out of projects are used as inputs in financial models such as internal rate of return, and net present value.
   - to determine problems with a business's liquidity. Being profitable does not necessarily mean being liquid. A company can fail because of a shortage of cash, even while profitable.
   - as an alternate measure of a business's profits when it is believed that accrual accounting concepts do not represent economic realities. For example, a company may be notionally profitable but generating little operational cash (as may be the case for a company that barters its products rather than selling for cash.) In such a case, the company may be deriving additional operating cash by issuing shares evaluating default risk, re-investment requirements, etc.

Chapter 14. Development Team Management

_____ is a generic term used differently depending on the context. It may be defined by users for their own purposes.

a. Sweat equity
b. Gross profit
c. Gross profit margin
d. Cash flow

5. An _____ is a person who has possession of an enterprise and assumes significant accountability for the inherent risks and the outcome. It is an ambitious leader who combines land, labor, and capital to create and market new goods or services. The term is a loanword from French and was first defined by the Irish economist Richard Cantillon.

a. A Stake in the Outcome
b. Entrepreneur
c. AAAI
d. A4e

6. The process of _____ involves the introduction of a good or service that is new or substantially improved. This includes, but is not limited to, improvements in functional characteristics, technical abilities, or ease of use.

a. Job enlargement
b. Letter of resignation
c. Product innovation
d. Service-profit chain

7. '_____ is a conflict among the roles corresponding to two or more statuses.'

_____ is a special form of social conflict that takes place when one is forced to take on two different and incompatible roles at the same time. Consider the example of a doctor who is himself a patient, or who must decide whether he should be present for his daughter's birthday party (in his role as 'father') or attend an ailing patient (as 'doctor'.) (Also compare the psychological concept of cognitive dissonance.)

a. Social network analysis
b. Self-disclosure
c. Role conflict
d. Soft skill

Chapter 14. Development Team Management

8. In decision theory and estimation theory, the _____ of an estimator, $\hat{\theta}$, of an unknown parameter of the distribution, θ, is the expected value of the loss function

$$R(\theta, \hat{\theta}) = \mathbb{E}_\theta L(\theta, \hat{\theta}) = \int L(\theta, \hat{\theta})\, dP_\theta.$$

where dP_θ is a probability measure parametrized by θ.

- For a scalar parameter θ and a quadratic loss function,

$$L(\theta, \hat{\theta}) = (\theta - \hat{\theta})^2$$

    the _____ function becomes the mean squared error of the estimate,

$$R(\theta, \hat{\theta}) = E_\theta(\theta - \hat{\theta})^2$$

- In density estimation, the unknown parameter is probability density itself. The loss function is typically chosen to be a norm in an appropriate function space. For example, for L^2 norm,

$$L(f, \hat{f}) = \|f - \hat{f}\|_2^2$$

    the _____ function becomes the mean integrated squared error

$$R(f, \hat{f}) = E\|f - \hat{f}\|^2$$

a. Risk aversion
b. Financial modeling
c. Risk
d. Linear model

9. _____ is a recursive process where two or more people or organizations work together in an intersection of common goals -- for example, an intellectual endeavor that is creative in nature--by sharing knowledge, learning and building consensus. _____ does not require leadership and can sometimes bring better results through decentralization and egalitarianism. In particular, teams that work collaboratively can obtain greater resources, recognition and reward when facing competition for finite resources. _____ is also present in opposing goals exhibiting the notion of adversarial _____, though this is not a common case for using the term.

Chapter 14. Development Team Management

a. 1990 Clean Air Act
b. 28-hour day
c. Collectivism
d. Collaboration

10. _____ is the term used to describe a situation where different entities cooperate advantageously for a final outcome. Simply defined, it means that the whole is greater than the sum of the individual parts. Although the whole will be greater than each individual part, this is not the concept of _____.

a. 1990 Clean Air Act
b. Synergy
c. 33 Strategies of War
d. 28-hour day

11. _____ refers to increasing the spiritual, political, social or economic strength of individuals and communities. It often involves the empowered developing confidence in their own capacities.

The term Human _____ covers a vast landscape of meanings, interpretations, definitions and disciplines ranging from psychology and philosophy to the highly commercialized Self-Help industry and Motivational sciences.

a. A Stake in the Outcome
b. A4e
c. Empowerment
d. AAAI

12. _____ is a civil designation for persons who are incorporated in a fixed or permanent way to a society or group: regular member of the working staff, permanent staff distinguished from a supernumerary.

The term '_____' and its counterpart, 'supernumerary,' originated in Spanish and Latin American academy and government; it is now also used in countries all over the world, such as France, the U.S., England, Italy, etc.

There are _____ members of surgical organizations, of universities, of gastronomical associations, etc.

a. Adam Smith
b. Numerary
c. Abraham Harold Maslow
d. Affiliation

Chapter 14. Development Team Management

13. The _____ captures an expanded spectrum of values and criteria for measuring organizational success: economic, ecological and social. With the ratification of the United Nations and ICLEI _____ standard for urban and community accounting in early 2007, this became the dominant approach to public sector full cost accounting. Similar UN standards apply to natural capital and human capital measurement to assist in measurements required by _____, e.g. the ecoBudget standard for reporting ecological footprint.
   a. 33 Strategies of War
   b. 1990 Clean Air Act
   c. 28-hour day
   d. Triple bottom line

14. _____ for short is a descriptive term for certain executives in a business operation. It is also a formal title held by some business executives, most commonly in the hospitality industry.

   A _____ has broad, overall responsibility for a business or organization. Whereas a manager may be responsible for one functional area, the _____ is responsible for all areas.

   a. Chief technology officer
   b. Managing director
   c. Chief knowledge officer
   d. General manager

15. A _____ is one scenario provided for evaluation by respondents in a Choice Experiment. Responses are collected and used to create a Choice Model. Respondents are usually provided with a series of differing _____s for evaluation.
   a. Pairwise comparison
   b. Choice Set
   c. Thurstone scale
   d. Computerized classification test

16. A _____ is a professional in the field of project management. _____s can have the responsibility of the planning, execution, and closing of any project, typically relating to construction industry, architecture, computer networking, telecommunications or software development.

   Many other fields in the production, design and service industries also have _____s.

Chapter 14. Development Team Management

a. Work package
b. Project engineer
c. Project manager
d. Project management

17. A _____ is someone who helps a group of people understand their common objectives and assists them to plan to achieve them without taking a particular position in the discussion. The _____ will try to assist the group in achieving a consensus on any disagreements that preexist or emerge in the meeting so that it has a strong basis for future action. The role has been likened to that of a midwife who assists in the process of birth but is not the producer of the end result.

a. 28-hour day
b. 1990 Clean Air Act
c. 33 Strategies of War
d. Facilitator

18. A _____ or business method is a collection of related, structured activities or tasks that produce a specific service or product (serve a particular goal) for a particular customer or customers. It often can be visualized with a flowchart as a sequence of activities.

There are three types of _____es:

1. Management processes, the processes that govern the operation of a system. Typical management processes include 'Corporate Governance' and 'Strategic Management'.
2. Operational processes, processes that constitute the core business and create the primary value stream. Typical operational processes are Purchasing, Manufacturing, Marketing, and Sales.
3. Supporting processes, which support the core processes. Examples include Accounting, Recruitment, Technical support.

A _____ begins with a customer's need and ends with a customer's need fulfillment. Process oriented organizations break down the barriers of structural departments and try to avoid functional silos.

a. Business process
b. 1990 Clean Air Act
c. 33 Strategies of War
d. 28-hour day

19. _____ has been described as the 'process of social influence in which one person can enlist the aid and support of others in the accomplishment of a common task' . A definition more inclusive of followers comes from Alan Keith of Genentech who said '_____ is ultimately about creating a way for people to contribute to making something extraordinary happen.'

Chapter 14. Development Team Management

_____ is one of the most salient aspects of the organizational context. However, defining _____ has been challenging.

a. 1990 Clean Air Act
b. 28-hour day
c. Situational leadership
d. Leadership

20. _____ is generally a team of individuals at the highest level of organizational management who have the day-to-day responsibilities of managing a corporation. There are most often higher levels of responsibility, such as a board of directors and those who own the company (shareholders), but they focus on managing the _____ instead of the day-to-day activities of the business.

They are sometimes referred to, within corporations, as top management, upper management, higher management, or simply seniors.

a. Senior management
b. Crisis management
c. Management development
d. Functional management

21. _____ refers to the long-term management of intractable conflicts. It is the label for the variety of ways by which people handle grievances--standing up for what they consider to be right and against what they consider to be wrong. Those ways include such diverse phenomena as gossip, ridicule, lynching, terrorism, warfare, feuding, genocide, law, mediation, and avoidance.

a. 1990 Clean Air Act
b. 28-hour day
c. 33 Strategies of War
d. Conflict management

22. Various _____ can be employed dependent on the culture of the business, the nature of the task, the nature of the workforce and the personality and skills of the leaders. This idea was further developed by Robert Tannenbaum and Warren H. Schmidt (1958, 1973) who argued that the style of leadership is dependent upon the prevailing circumstance; therefore leaders should exercise a range of leadership styles and should deploy them as appropriate.

An Autocratic or authoritarian manager makes all the decisions, keeping the information and decision making among the senior management.

a. 33 Strategies of War
b. 1990 Clean Air Act
c. 28-hour day
d. Management styles

23. _____ is the probability that an individual will keep his or her job; a job with a high level of _____ is such that a person with the job would have a small chance of becoming unemployed.

_____ is dependent on economy, prevailing business conditions, and the individual's personal skills. It has been found that people have more _____ in times of economic expansion and less in times of a recession.

a. Job security
b. Multiple careers
c. Just cause
d. Hygiene factors

24. _____ refers to techniques, processes and tools for organizing and coordinating a group of individuals working towards a common goal--i.e. a team.

Several well-known approaches to _____ have come out of academic work. Examples include the Belbin Team Inventory by Meredith Belbin, a method to identify the different types of personalities within teams, and Ken Blanchard's description of 'High Performing Teams'.

a. 33 Strategies of War
b. Team management
c. 1990 Clean Air Act
d. 28-hour day

Chapter 15. Product Use Testing

1. _____ is an integrated communications-based process through which individuals and communities discover that existing and newly-identified needs and wants may be satisfied by the products and services of others.

   _____ is defined by the American _____ Association as the activity, set of institutions, and processes for creating, communicating, delivering, and exchanging offerings that have value for customers, clients, partners, and society at large. The term developed from the original meaning which referred literally to going to market, as in shopping, or going to a market to buy or sell goods or services.

   a. Customer relationship management
   b. Market development
   c. Marketing
   d. Disruptive technology

2. In physics, and more specifically kinematics, _____ is the change in velocity over time. Because velocity is a vector, it can change in two ways: a change in magnitude and/or a change in direction. In one dimension, _____ is the rate at which something speeds up or slows down.

   a. A4e
   b. AAAI
   c. A Stake in the Outcome
   d. Acceleration

3. Marketing research is a form of business research and is generally divided into two categories: consumer _____ and business-to-business (B2B) _____, which was previously known as industrial marketing research. Consumer marketing research studies the buying habits of individual people while business-to-business marketing research investigates the markets for products sold by one business to another.

   Consumer _____ is a form of applied sociology that concentrates on understanding the behaviours, whims and preferences, of consumers in a market-based economy, and aims to understand the effects and comparative success of marketing campaigns.

   a. Questionnaire
   b. Questionnaire construction
   c. Mystery shoppers
   d. Market research

4. The term _____ in logic applies to arguments or statements.

An argument is valid if and only if the truth of its premises entails the truth of its conclusion, it would be self-contradictory to affirm the premises and deny the conclusion. The corresponding conditional of a valid argument is a logical truth and the negation of its corresponding conditional is a contradiction.

Chapter 15. Product Use Testing

a. Simplification
b. Fuzzy logic
c. 1990 Clean Air Act
d. Validity

5. _____ is one of the managerial functions like planning, organizing, staffing and directing. It is an important function because it helps to check the errors and to take the corrective action so that deviation from standards are minimized and stated goals of the organization are achieved in desired manner. According to modern concepts, _____ is a foreseeing action whereas earlier concept of _____ was used only when errors were detected. _____ in management means setting standards, measuring actual performance and taking corrective action.

a. Schedule of reinforcement
b. Turnover
c. Decision tree pruning
d. Control

6. _____ is a type of a rating scale designed to measure the connotative meaning of objects, events, and concepts. The connotations are used to derive the attitude towards the given object, event or concept.

Osgood's _____ was designed to measure the connotative meaning of concepts.

a. Computerized classification test
b. Pairwise comparison
c. Semantic differential
d. Multistage testing

7. _____ is an advertisement in which a particular product specifically mentions a competitor by name for the express purpose of showing why the competitor is inferior to the product naming it.

This should not be confused with parody advertisements, where a fictional product is being advertised for the purpose of poking fun at the particular advertisement, nor should it be confused with the use of a coined brand name for the purpose of comparing the product without actually naming an actual competitor. ('Wikipedia tastes better and is less filling than the Encyclopedia Galactica.')

In the 1980s, during what has been referred to as the cola wars, soft-drink manufacturer Pepsi ran a series of advertisements where people, caught on hidden camera, in a blind taste test, chose Pepsi over rival Coca-Cola.

a. 1990 Clean Air Act
b. Comparative advertising
c. 33 Strategies of War
d. 28-hour day

8. _____ is the science, art and technology of enclosing or protecting products for distribution, storage, sale, and use. _____ also refers to the process of design, evaluation, and production of packages. _____ can be described as a coordinated system of preparing goods for transport, warehousing, logistics, sale, and end use.

a. Supply chain management
b. Wholesalers
c. Supply chain
d. Packaging

9. _____-model (SCOR(r)) is a process reference model developed by the management consulting firm PRTM and AMR Research and endorsed by the Supply-Chain Council (SCC) as the cross-industry de facto standard diagnostic tool for supply chain management. SCOR enables users to address, improve, and communicate supply chain management practices within and between all interested parties in the Extended Enterprise.

SCOR(r) is a management tool, spanning from the supplier's supplier to the customer's customer. The model has been developed by the members of the Council on a volunteer basis to describe the business activities associated with all phases of satisfying a customer's demand.

a. Supply chain management software
b. Delayed differentiation
c. Supply Chain Risk Management
d. Supply-Chain Operations Reference

10. _____ is a broad label that refers to any individuals or households that use goods and services generated within the economy. The concept of a _____ is used in different contexts, so that the usage and significance of the term may vary.

Typically when business people and economists talk of _____s they are talking about person as _____, an aggregated commodity item with little individuality other than that expressed in the buy/not-buy decision.

a. 33 Strategies of War
b. 1990 Clean Air Act
c. 28-hour day
d. Consumer

Chapter 16. Strategic Launch Planning

1. _____ is an organization's process of defining its strategy and making decisions on allocating its resources to pursue this strategy, including its capital and people. Various business analysis techniques can be used in _____, including SWOT analysis (Strengths, Weaknesses, Opportunities, and Threats) and PEST analysis (Political, Economic, Social, and Technological analysis) or STEER analysis involving Socio-cultural, Technological, Economic, Ecological, and Regulatory factors and EPISTEL (Environment, Political, Informatic, Social, Technological, Economic and Legal)

_____ is the formal consideration of an organization's future course. All _____ deals with at least one of three key questions:

1. 'What do we do?'
2. 'For whom do we do it?'
3. 'How do we excel?'

In business _____, the third question is better phrased 'How can we beat or avoid competition?'. (Bradford and Duncan, page 1.)

a. 1990 Clean Air Act
b. 28-hour day
c. 33 Strategies of War
d. Strategic planning

2. In economics, _____ is the desire to own something and the ability to pay for it. The term _____ signifies the ability or the willingness to buy a particular commodity at a given point of time.
a. 28-hour day
b. 33 Strategies of War
c. 1990 Clean Air Act
d. Demand

3. In finance, an _____ is a contract between a buyer and a seller that gives the buyer the right--but not the obligation-- to buy or to sell a particular asset (the underlying asset) at a later day at an agreed price. In return for granting the _____, the seller collects a payment (the premium) from the buyer. A call _____ gives the buyer the right to buy the underlying asset; a put _____ gives the buyer of the _____ the right to sell the underlying asset.
a. AAAI
b. A Stake in the Outcome
c. A4e
d. Option

4. _____ is, in very basic words, a position a firm occupies against its competitors.

According to Michael Porter, the three methods for creating a sustainable _____ are through:

Chapter 16. Strategic Launch Planning 81

1. Cost leadership

2. Differentiation

3. Focus (economics)

   a. 1990 Clean Air Act
   b. 28-hour day
   c. Theory Z
   d. Competitive advantage

5. There are many important decisions about product and service development and marketing. In the process of product development and marketing we should focus on strategic decisions about product attributes, product branding, product packaging, product labeling and product support services. But product strategy also calls for building a _____.
   a. Marketing strategy
   b. Product bundling
   c. Context analysis
   d. Product line

6. In economics, business, retail, and accounting, a _____ is the value of money that has been used up to produce something, and hence is not available for use anymore. In economics, a _____ is an alternative that is given up as a result of a decision. In business, the _____ may be one of acquisition, in which case the amount of money expended to acquire it is counted as _____.
   a. Fixed costs
   b. Cost allocation
   c. Cost overrun
   d. Cost

7. _____ is an integrated communications-based process through which individuals and communities discover that existing and newly-identified needs and wants may be satisfied by the products and services of others.

_____ is defined by the American _____ Association as the activity, set of institutions, and processes for creating, communicating, delivering, and exchanging offerings that have value for customers, clients, partners, and society at large. The term developed from the original meaning which referred literally to going to market, as in shopping, or going to a market to buy or sell goods or services.

a. Disruptive technology
b. Marketing
c. Customer relationship management
d. Market development

8. A _____ strategy is the planned method of delivering goods or services to a target market and distributing them there. When importing or exporting services, it refers to establishing and managing contracts in a foreign country.

Many companies successfully operate in a niche market without ever expanding into new markets.

a. Market entry
b. Psychological pricing
c. Foreign ownership
d. Horizontal integration

9. A _____ is a group of people or organizations sharing one or more characteristics that cause them to have similar product and/or service needs. A true _____ meets all of the following criteria: it is distinct from other segments (different segments have different needs), it is homogeneous within the segment (exhibits common needs); it responds similarly to a market stimulus, and it can be reached by a market intervention. The term is also used when consumers with identical product and/or service needs are divided up into groups so they can be charged different amounts.

a. Context analysis
b. Customer relationship management
c. SWOT analysis
d. Market segment

10. _____ or _____ data refers to selected population characteristics as used in government, marketing or opinion research, or the _____ profiles used in such research. Note the distinction from the term 'demography' Commonly-used _____s include race, age, income, disabilities, mobility (in terms of travel time to work or number of vehicles available), educational attainment, home ownership, employment status, and even location.

a. Adam Smith
b. Abraham Harold Maslow
c. Affiliation
d. Demographic

11. A _____ is a research instrument consisting of a series of questions and other prompts for the purpose of gathering information from respondents. Although they are often designed for statistical analysis of the responses, this is not always the case. The _____ was invented by Sir Francis Galton.

a. Mystery shoppers
b. Questionnaire
c. Questionnaire construction
d. Structured interview

12. _____, in marketing, manufacturing, call centres and management, is the use of flexible computer-aided manufacturing systems to produce custom output. Those systems combine the low unit costs of mass production processes with the flexibility of individual customization.

'_____' is the new frontier in business competition for both manufacturing and service industries.

a. 28-hour day
b. 33 Strategies of War
c. 1990 Clean Air Act
d. Mass customization

13. Marketing research is a form of business research and is generally divided into two categories: consumer _____ and business-to-business (B2B) _____, which was previously known as industrial marketing research. Consumer marketing research studies the buying habits of individual people while business-to-business marketing research investigates the markets for products sold by one business to another.

Consumer _____ is a form of applied sociology that concentrates on understanding the behaviours, whims and preferences, of consumers in a market-based economy, and aims to understand the effects and comparative success of marketing campaigns.

a. Questionnaire construction
b. Market research
c. Mystery shoppers
d. Questionnaire

14. _____ is the process by which a new idea or new product is accepted by the market. The rate of _____ is the speed that the new idea spreads from one consumer to the next. Adoption is similar to _____ except that it deals with the psychological processes an individual goes through, rather than an aggregate market process.
a. Value chain
b. Mass marketing
c. Category management
d. Diffusion

Chapter 16. Strategic Launch Planning

15. _____ is a term developed by Eric von Hippel in 1986. His definition for _____ is:

    1. _____s face needs that will be general in a marketplace - but face them months or years before the bulk of that marketplace encounters them, and
    2. _____s are positioned to benefit significantly by obtaining a solution to those needs.

    In other words: _____s are users of a product that currently experience needs still unknown to the public and who also benefit greatly if they obtain a solution to these needs.

    The _____ Method is a market research tool that may be used by companies and / or individuals seeking to develop breakthrough products. _____ methodology was originally developed by Dr. Eric von Hippel of the Massachusetts Institute of Technology (MIT) and first described in the July 1986 issue of the Journal of Management Science.

    a. 33 Strategies of War
    b. Lead user
    c. 1990 Clean Air Act
    d. 28-hour day

16. In economics, _____ is a measure of the relative satisfaction from consumption of various goods and services. Given this measure, one may speak meaningfully of increasing or decreasing _____, and thereby explain economic behavior in terms of attempts to increase one's _____. For illustrative purposes, changes in _____ are sometimes expressed in units called utils.
    a. Indirect utility function
    b. A Stake in the Outcome
    c. Ordinal utility
    d. Utility

17. In probability theory, a probability distribution is called _____ if its cumulative distribution function is _____. This is equivalent to saying that for random variables X with the distribution in question, Pr[X = a] = 0 for all real numbers a, i.e.: the probability that X attains the value a is zero, for any number a. If the distribution of X is _____ then X is called a _____ random variable.
    a. Decision tree pruning
    b. Pay Band
    c. Connectionist expert systems
    d. Continuous

18. In marketing, _____ has come to mean the process by which marketers try to create an image or identity in the minds of their target market for its product, brand, or organization. It is the 'relative competitive comparison' their product occupies in a given market as perceived by the target market.

Re-_____ involves changing the identity of a product, relative to the identity of competing products, in the collective minds of the target market.

a. Customer analytics
b. Context analysis
c. PEST analysis
d. Positioning

19. _____ is an advertisement in which a particular product specifically mentions a competitor by name for the express purpose of showing why the competitor is inferior to the product naming it.

This should not be confused with parody advertisements, where a fictional product is being advertised for the purpose of poking fun at the particular advertisement, nor should it be confused with the use of a coined brand name for the purpose of comparing the product without actually naming an actual competitor. ('Wikipedia tastes better and is less filling than the Encyclopedia Galactica.')

In the 1980s, during what has been referred to as the cola wars, soft-drink manufacturer Pepsi ran a series of advertisements where people, caught on hidden camera, in a blind taste test, chose Pepsi over rival Coca-Cola.

a. Comparative advertising
b. 1990 Clean Air Act
c. 33 Strategies of War
d. 28-hour day

20. A _____ is a distinctive sign or indicator used by an individual, business organization, or other legal entity to identify that the products and/or services to consumers with which the _____ appears originate from a unique source and to distinguish its products or services from those of other entities.
a. Succession planning
b. Virtual team
c. Kanban
d. Trademark

21. A _____ is a name or trademark connected with a product or producer. _____s have become increasingly important components of culture and the economy, now being described as 'cultural accessories and personal philosophies'.

Some people distinguish the psychological aspect of a _____ from the experiential aspect.

a. Brand loyalty
b. Brand extension
c. Brand awareness
d. Brand

22. Descriptive _____ assist in describing the distinguishable selling point(s) of the product to the customer (eg Snap Crackle ' Pop or Bitter Lemon.)

Associative _____ provide the customer with an associated word for what the product promises to do or be (e.g. Walkman, Sensodyne or Natrel)

Finally, Freestanding _____ have no links or ties to either descriptions or associations of use. (eg Mars Bar or Pantene)

The act of associating a product or service with a brand has become part of pop culture.

a. Brand awareness
b. Brand extension
c. Brand image
d. Brand names

23. _____ consists of the mental process of thinking involved with the process of judging the merits of multiple options and selecting one of them for action. Some simple examples include deciding whether to get up in the morning or go back to sleep, or selecting a given route for a journey. More complex examples (often decisions that affect what a person thinks or their core beliefs) include choosing a lifestyle, religious affiliation, or political position.

a. Choice
b. Groups decision making
c. Trade study
d. Championship mobilization

24. _____ or brand stretching is a marketing strategy in which a firm marketing a product with a well-developed image uses the same brand name in a different product category. Organizations use this strategy to increase and leverage brand equity (definition: the net worth and long-term sustainability just from the renowned name.) An example of a _____ is Jello-gelatin creating Jello pudding pops.

a. Brand image
b. Channel conflict
c. Brand awareness
d. Brand extension

Chapter 16. Strategic Launch Planning

25. _____, in strategic management and marketing is, according to Carlton O'Neal, the percentage or proportion of the total available market or market segment that is being serviced by a company. It can be expressed as a company's sales revenue (from that market) divided by the total sales revenue available in that market. It can also be expressed as a company's unit sales volume (in a market) divided by the total volume of units sold in that market.
    a. Business-to-business
    b. Marketing plan
    c. Green marketing
    d. Market share

26. _____ has been described as the 'process of social influence in which one person can enlist the aid and support of others in the accomplishment of a common task' . A definition more inclusive of followers comes from Alan Keith of Genentech who said '_____ is ultimately about creating a way for people to contribute to making something extraordinary happen.'

    _____ is one of the most salient aspects of the organizational context. However, defining _____ has been challenging.

    a. 1990 Clean Air Act
    b. Leadership
    c. 28-hour day
    d. Situational leadership

27. A _____ is one scenario provided for evaluation by respondents in a Choice Experiment. Responses are collected and used to create a Choice Model. Respondents are usually provided with a series of differing _____s for evaluation.
    a. Pairwise comparison
    b. Thurstone scale
    c. Computerized classification test
    d. Choice Set

28. _____ is the science, art and technology of enclosing or protecting products for distribution, storage, sale, and use. _____ also refers to the process of design, evaluation, and production of packages. _____ can be described as a coordinated system of preparing goods for transport, warehousing, logistics, sale, and end use.
    a. Packaging
    b. Supply chain management
    c. Supply chain
    d. Wholesalers

Chapter 17. Implementation of the Strategic Plan

1. _____ Management is the succession of strategies used by management as a product goes through its _____. The conditions in which a product is sold changes over time and must be managed as it moves through its succession of stages.

   The _____ goes through many phases, involves many professional disciplines, and requires many skills, tools and processes.

   a. Product life cycle
   b. Golden handshake
   c. Strategic Alliance
   d. Job hunting

2. Many negative _____ are related to the environmental consequences of production and use

   - Systemic risk describes the risks to the overall economy arising from the risks which the banking system takes. That the private costs of banking failure may be smaller than the social costs justifies banking regulations, although regulations could create a moral hazard.

   - Anthropogenic climate change is attributed to greenhouse gas emissions from burning oil, gas, and coal. Global warming has been ranked as the #1 externality of all economic activity, in the magnitude of potential harms and yet remains unmitigated.

   a. AAAI
   b. A Stake in the Outcome
   c. Externalities
   d. A4e

3. A _____ is a formal relationship between two or more parties to pursue a set of agreed upon goals or to meet a critical business need while remaining independent organizations.

   Partners may provide the _____ with resources such as products, distribution channels, manufacturing capability, project funding, capital equipment, knowledge, expertise, or intellectual property. The alliance is a cooperation or collaboration which aims for a synergy where each partner hopes that the benefits from the alliance will be greater than those from individual efforts.

   a. Farmshoring
   b. Process automation
   c. Golden parachute
   d. Strategic alliance

Chapter 17. Implementation of the Strategic Plan

4. _____ is an integrated communications-based process through which individuals and communities discover that existing and newly-identified needs and wants may be satisfied by the products and services of others.

_____ is defined by the American _____ Association as the activity, set of institutions, and processes for creating, communicating, delivering, and exchanging offerings that have value for customers, clients, partners, and society at large. The term developed from the original meaning which referred literally to going to market, as in shopping, or going to a market to buy or sell goods or services.

   a. Market development
   b. Marketing
   c. Customer relationship management
   d. Disruptive technology

5. In economics, business, retail, and accounting, a _____ is the value of money that has been used up to produce something, and hence is not available for use anymore. In economics, a _____ is an alternative that is given up as a result of a decision. In business, the _____ may be one of acquisition, in which case the amount of money expended to acquire it is counted as _____.
   a. Fixed costs
   b. Cost allocation
   c. Cost overrun
   d. Cost

6. _____ is an economic concept with commonplace familiarity. It is the price that a good or service is offered at, or will fetch, in the marketplace. It is of interest mainly in the study of microeconomics.
   a. 1990 Clean Air Act
   b. 33 Strategies of War
   c. 28-hour day
   d. Market price

7. In economics, _____ is a measure of the relative satisfaction from consumption of various goods and services. Given this measure, one may speak meaningfully of increasing or decreasing _____, and thereby explain economic behavior in terms of attempts to increase one's _____. For illustrative purposes, changes in _____ are sometimes expressed in units called utils.
   a. Ordinal utility
   b. Utility
   c. Indirect utility function
   d. A Stake in the Outcome

Chapter 18. Market Testing

1. A _____, in the field of business and marketing, is a geographic region or demographic group used to gauge the viability of a product or service in the mass market prior to a wide scale roll-out. The criteria used to judge the acceptability of a _____ region or group include:

    1. a population that is demographically similar to the proposed target market; and
    2. relative isolation from densely populated media markets so that advertising to the test audience can be efficient and economical.

The _____ ideally aims to duplicate 'everything' - promotion and distribution as well as `product' - on a smaller scale. The technique replicates, typically in one area, what is planned to occur in a national launch; and the results are very carefully monitored, so that they can be extrapolated to projected national results. The `area' may be any one of the following:

- Television area

internet online test

- Test town
- Residential neighborhood
- Test site

A number of decisions have to be taken about any _____:

- Which _____?
- What is to be tested?
- How long a test?
- What are the success criteria?

The simple go or no-go decision, together with the related reduction of risk, is normally the main justification for the expense of _____s. At the same time, however, such _____s can be used to test specific elements of a new product's marketing mix; possibly the version of the product itself, the promotional message and media spend, the distribution channels and the price.

a. 1990 Clean Air Act
b. 28-hour day
c. Test market
d. 33 Strategies of War

2. _____ is an integrated communications-based process through which individuals and communities discover that existing and newly-identified needs and wants may be satisfied by the products and services of others.

_____ is defined by the American _____ Association as the activity, set of institutions, and processes for creating, communicating, delivering, and exchanging offerings that have value for customers, clients, partners, and society at large. The term developed from the original meaning which referred literally to going to market, as in shopping, or going to a market to buy or sell goods or services.

a. Disruptive technology
b. Market development
c. Customer relationship management
d. Marketing

3. In business and engineering, new _____ is the term used to describe the complete process of bringing a new product or service to market. There are two parallel paths involved in the NProduct development process: one involves the idea generation, product design, and detail engineering; the other involves market research and marketing analysis. Companies typically see new _____ as the first stage in generating and commercializing new products within the overall strategic process of product life cycle management used to maintain or grow their market share.

a. 28-hour day
b. 33 Strategies of War
c. 1990 Clean Air Act
d. Product development

4. In economics, business, retail, and accounting, a _____ is the value of money that has been used up to produce something, and hence is not available for use anymore. In economics, a _____ is an alternative that is given up as a result of a decision. In business, the _____ may be one of acquisition, in which case the amount of money expended to acquire it is counted as _____.

a. Cost
b. Cost overrun
c. Cost allocation
d. Fixed costs

5. _____ is a business management strategy aimed at embedding awareness of quality in all organizational processes. _____ has been widely used in manufacturing, education, hospitals, call centers, government, and service industries, as well as NASA space and science programs.

As defined by the International Organization for Standardization (ISO):

'_____ is a management approach for an organization, centered on quality, based on the participation of all its members and aiming at long-term success through customer satisfaction, and benefits to all members of the organization and to society.' ISO 8402:1994

One major aim is to reduce variation from every process so that greater consistency of effort is obtained. (Royse, D., Thyer, B., Padgett D., ' Logan T., 2006)

a. 28-hour day
b. 1990 Clean Air Act
c. Total quality management
d. Quality management

6. _____ can be considered to have three main components: quality control, quality assurance and quality improvement. _____ is focused not only on product quality, but also the means to achieve it. _____ therefore uses quality assurance and control of processes as well as products to achieve more consistent quality.

a. 28-hour day
b. Total quality management
c. 1990 Clean Air Act
d. Quality management

7. The _____ Automobile Company is an automobile manufacturer based in Wolfsburg, Germany, and is the original brand within the _____ Group, as well as the largest brand by sales volume.

_____ means 'people's car' in German, in which it is pronounced . Its current tagline or slogan is Das Auto .

a. Turnover
b. Rate of return
c. Competence-based Strategic Management
d. Volkswagen

8. _____ is an adjective for experience-based techniques that help in problem solving, learning and discovery. A _____ method is particularly used to rapidly come to a solution that is hoped to be close to the best possible answer, or 'optimal solution'. _____s are 'rules of thumb', educated guesses, intuitive judgments or simply common sense.

a. 28-hour day
b. Representativeness
c. 1990 Clean Air Act
d. Heuristic

9. _____ is a sub-discipline and type of marketing. There are two main definitional characteristics which distinguish it from other types of marketing. The first is that it attempts to send its messages directly to consumers, without the use of intervening media.

Chapter 18. Market Testing

a. 1990 Clean Air Act
b. 28-hour day
c. Guthy-Renker
d. Direct marketing

10. _____ is a broad label that refers to any individuals or households that use goods and services generated within the economy. The concept of a _____ is used in different contexts, so that the usage and significance of the term may vary.

Typically when business people and economists talk of _____s they are talking about person as _____, an aggregated commodity item with little individuality other than that expressed in the buy/not-buy decision.

a. 28-hour day
b. 33 Strategies of War
c. Consumer
d. 1990 Clean Air Act

11. _____ is an advertisement in which a particular product specifically mentions a competitor by name for the express purpose of showing why the competitor is inferior to the product naming it.

This should not be confused with parody advertisements, where a fictional product is being advertised for the purpose of poking fun at the particular advertisement, nor should it be confused with the use of a coined brand name for the purpose of comparing the product without actually naming an actual competitor. ('Wikipedia tastes better and is less filling than the Encyclopedia Galactica.')

In the 1980s, during what has been referred to as the cola wars, soft-drink manufacturer Pepsi ran a series of advertisements where people, caught on hidden camera, in a blind taste test, chose Pepsi over rival Coca-Cola.

a. 28-hour day
b. 1990 Clean Air Act
c. Comparative advertising
d. 33 Strategies of War

12. An _____ is software that attempts to reproduce the performance of one or more human experts, most commonly in a specific problem domain, and is a traditional application and/or subfield of artificial intelligence. A wide variety of methods can be used to simulate the performance of the expert however common to most or all are 1) the creation of a so-called 'knowledgebase' which uses some knowledge representation formalism to capture the Subject Matter Experts (SME) knowledge and 2) a process of gathering that knowledge from the SME and codifying it according to the formalism, which is called knowledge engineering. _____s may or may not have learning components but a third common element is that once the system is developed it is proven by being placed in the same real world problem solving situation as the human SME, typically as an aid to human workers or a supplement to some information system.

a. A Stake in the Outcome
b. AAAI
c. Expert system
d. A4e

13. In decision theory and estimation theory, the _____ of an estimator, $\hat{\theta}$, of an unknown parameter of the distribution, θ, is the expected value of the loss function

$$R(\theta, \hat{\theta}) = \mathbb{E}_\theta L(\theta, \hat{\theta}) = \int L(\theta, \hat{\theta}) \, dP_\theta.$$

where dP_θ is a probability measure parametrized by θ.

- For a scalar parameter θ and a quadratic loss function,

$$L(\theta, \hat{\theta}) = (\theta - \hat{\theta})^2$$

the _____ function becomes the mean squared error of the estimate,

$$R(\theta, \hat{\theta}) = E_\theta(\theta - \hat{\theta})^2$$

- In density estimation, the unknown parameter is probability density itself. The loss function is typically chosen to be a norm in an appropriate function space. For example, for L^2 norm,

$$L(f, \hat{f}) = \|f - \hat{f}\|_2^2$$

the _____ function becomes the mean integrated squared error

$$R(f, \hat{f}) = E\|f - \hat{f}\|^2$$

a. Linear model
b. Financial modeling
c. Risk aversion
d. Risk

14. _____ is a form of communication that typically attempts to persuade potential customers to purchase or to consume more of a particular brand of product or service. 'While now central to the contemporary global economy and the reproduction of global production networks, it is only quite recently that _____ has been more than a marginal influence on patterns of sales and production. The formation of modern _____ was intimately bound up with the emergence of new forms of monopoly capitalism around the end of the 19th and beginning of the 20th century as one element in corporate strategies to create, organize and where possible control markets, especially for mass produced consumer goods.
   a. A Stake in the Outcome
   b. Advertising
   c. AAAI
   d. A4e

Chapter 19. Launch Management

1. A _____ is a plan devised for a specific situation when things could go wrong. _____s are often devised by governments or businesses who want to be prepared for anything that could happen. They are sometimes known as 'Back-up plans', 'Worst-case scenario plans' or 'Plan B'.
    a. Contingency plan
    b. 1990 Clean Air Act
    c. 33 Strategies of War
    d. 28-hour day

2. _____ is one of the managerial functions like planning, organizing, staffing and directing. It is an important function because it helps to check the errors and to take the corrective action so that deviation from standards are minimized and stated goals of the organization are achieved in desired manner. According to modern concepts, _____ is a foreseeing action whereas earlier concept of _____ was used only when errors were detected. _____ in management means setting standards, measuring actual performance and taking corrective action.
    a. Schedule of reinforcement
    b. Decision tree pruning
    c. Control
    d. Turnover

3. _____ is a broad label that refers to any individuals or households that use goods and services generated within the economy. The concept of a _____ is used in different contexts, so that the usage and significance of the term may vary.

    Typically when business people and economists talk of _____s they are talking about person as _____, an aggregated commodity item with little individuality other than that expressed in the buy/not-buy decision.

    a. 28-hour day
    b. 1990 Clean Air Act
    c. 33 Strategies of War
    d. Consumer

4. _____ is an integrated communications-based process through which individuals and communities discover that existing and newly-identified needs and wants may be satisfied by the products and services of others.

    _____ is defined by the American _____ Association as the activity, set of institutions, and processes for creating, communicating, delivering, and exchanging offerings that have value for customers, clients, partners, and society at large. The term developed from the original meaning which referred literally to going to market, as in shopping, or going to a market to buy or sell goods or services.

Chapter 19. Launch Management

a. Market development
b. Marketing
c. Customer relationship management
d. Disruptive technology

5. In game theory, an _____ is a set of moves or strategies taken by the players, or their payoffs resulting from the actions or strategies taken by all players. The two are complementary in that given knowledge of the set of strategies of all players, the final state of the game is known, as are any relevant payoffs. In a game where chance or a random event is involved, the _____ is not known from only the set of strategies, but is only realized when the random event(s) are realized.
   a. Outcome
   b. AAAI
   c. A Stake in the Outcome
   d. A4e

6. _____ refers to the movement of cash into or out of a business or financial product. It is usually measured during a specified, finite period of time. Measurement of _____ can be used

   - to determine a project's rate of return or value. The time of _____s into and out of projects are used as inputs in financial models such as internal rate of return, and net present value.
   - to determine problems with a business's liquidity. Being profitable does not necessarily mean being liquid. A company can fail because of a shortage of cash, even while profitable.
   - as an alternate measure of a business's profits when it is believed that accrual accounting concepts do not represent economic realities. For example, a company may be notionally profitable but generating little operational cash (as may be the case for a company that barters its products rather than selling for cash.) In such a case, the company may be deriving additional operating cash by issuing shares evaluating default risk, re-investment requirements, etc.

   _____ is a generic term used differently depending on the context. It may be defined by users for their own purposes.

   a. Gross profit margin
   b. Gross profit
   c. Sweat equity
   d. Cash flow

7. A _____ is a name or trademark connected with a product or producer. _____s have become increasingly important components of culture and the economy, now being described as 'cultural accessories and personal philosophies'.

Some people distinguish the psychological aspect of a _____ from the experiential aspect.

a. Brand awareness
b. Brand loyalty
c. Brand extension
d. Brand

Chapter 20. Public Policy Issues

1. A _____ is a process in which a potential employee is evaluated by an employer for prospective employment in their company, organization and was established in the late 16th century.

A _____ typically precedes the hiring decision, and is used to evaluate the candidate. The interview is usually preceded by the evaluation of submitted résumés from interested candidates, then selecting a small number of candidates for interviews.

   a. Split shift
   b. Job interview
   c. Payrolling
   d. Supported employment

2. A _____ is typically described as a deliberate plan of action to guide decisions and achieve rational outcome(s.) However, the term may also be used to denote what is actually done, even though it is unplanned.

The term may apply to government, private sector organizations and groups, and individuals.

   a. 1990 Clean Air Act
   b. Policy
   c. 33 Strategies of War
   d. 28-hour day

3. _____ is the area of law in which manufacturers, distributors, suppliers, retailers, and others who make products available to the public are held responsible for the injuries those products cause.

In the United States, the claims most commonly associated with _____ are negligence, strict liability, breach of warranty, and various consumer protection claims. The majority of _____ laws are determined at the state level and vary widely from state to state.

   a. Leave of absence
   b. Railway Labor Act
   c. Right-to-work laws
   d. Product liability

4. In decision theory and estimation theory, the _____ of an estimator, $\hat{\theta}$, of an unknown parameter of the distribution, θ, is the expected value of the loss function

$$R(\theta, \hat{\theta}) = \mathbb{E}_\theta L(\theta, \hat{\theta}) = \int L(\theta, \hat{\theta})\, dP_\theta.$$

where dP_θ is a probability measure parametrized by θ.

- For a scalar parameter θ and a quadratic loss function,

$$L(\theta, \hat{\theta}) = (\theta - \hat{\theta})^2$$

the _____ function becomes the mean squared error of the estimate,

$$R(\theta, \hat{\theta}) = E_\theta (\theta - \hat{\theta})^2$$

- In density estimation, the unknown parameter is probability density itself. The loss function is typically chosen to be a norm in an appropriate function space. For example, for L^2 norm,

$$L(f, \hat{f}) = \|f - \hat{f}\|_2^2$$

the _____ function becomes the mean integrated squared error

$$R(f, \hat{f}) = E\|f - \hat{f}\|^2$$

a. Financial modeling
b. Linear model
c. Risk aversion
d. Risk

5. _____ is a legal concept in the common law legal systems usually used to achieve compensation for injuries (not accidents.) _____ is a type of tort or delict (also known as a civil wrong.)
a. Diminishing returns
b. Mediation
c. Certificate of Incorporation
d. Negligence

Chapter 20. Public Policy Issues

6. An _____ is quite usually a standard guarantee from the seller of a product that specifies the extent to which the quality or performance of the product is assured and states the conditions under which the product can be returned, replaced, or repaired. It is often given in the form of a specific, written 'Warranty' document. However, a warranty may also arise by operation of law based upon the seller's description of the goods, and perhaps their source and quality, and any material deviation from that specification would violate the guarantee.
   a. A Stake in the Outcome
   b. A4e
   c. AAAI
   d. Express warranty

7. In common law jurisdictions, an _____ is a contract law term for certain assurances that are presumed to be made in the sale of products or real property, due to the circumstances of the sale. These assurances are characterized as warranties irrespective of whether the seller has expressly promised them orally or in writing. They include an _____ of fitness for a particular purpose, an _____ of merchantability for products, _____ of workmanlike quality for services, and an _____ of habitability for a home.
   a. A Stake in the Outcome
   b. AAAI
   c. A4e
   d. Implied warranty

8. The doctrine of _____ in contract law provides that a contract cannot confer rights or impose obligations arising under it on any person or agent except the parties to it.

The premise is that only parties to contracts should be able to sue to enforce their rights or claim damages as such. However, the doctrine has proven problematic due to its implications upon contracts made for the benefit of third parties who are unable to enforce the obligations of the contracting parties.

   a. Comprehensive Environmental Response, Compensation, and Liability Act
   b. Blue sky law
   c. Privity
   d. Privacy Act of 1974

9. _____ makes a person responsible for the damage and loss caused by his/her acts and omissions regardless of culpability. _____ is important in torts (especially product liability), corporations law, and criminal law.
   a. Ten year occupational employment projection
   b. Competency-based job descriptions
   c. Historiometry
   d. Strict liability

10. The _____ is an agency of the United States Department of Health and Human Services and is responsible for regulating and supervising the safety of foods, dietary supplements, drugs, vaccines, biological medical products, blood products, medical devices, radiation-emitting devices, veterinary products, and cosmetics. The FDA also enforces section 361 of the Public Health Service Act and the associated regulations, including sanitation requirements on interstate travel as well as specific rules for control of disease on products ranging from pet turtles to semen donations for assisted reproductive medicine techniques.

The FDA is an agency within the United States Department of Health and Human Services responsible for protecting and promoting the nation's public health.

   a. 1990 Clean Air Act
   b. 28-hour day
   c. 33 Strategies of War
   d. Food and Drug Administration

11. _____ was a writer, management consultant, and self-described 'social ecologist.' Widely considered to be 'the father of modern management,' his 39 books and countless scholarly and popular articles explored how humans are organized across all sectors of society--in business, government and the nonprofit world. His writings have predicted many of the major developments of the late twentieth century, including privatization and decentralization; the rise of Japan to economic world power; the decisive importance of marketing; and the emergence of the information society with its necessity of lifelong learning. In 1959, Drucker coined the term 'knowledge worker' and later in his life considered knowledge work productivity to be the next frontier of management.
   a. Debora L. Spar
   b. Chrissie Hynde
   c. Jacques Al-Salawat Nasruddin Nasser
   d. Peter Ferdinand Drucker

12. According to the American Marketing Association, _____ is the marketing of products that are presumed to be environmentally safe. Thus _____ incorporates a broad range of activities, including product modification, changes to the production process, packaging changes, as well as modifying advertising. Yet defining _____ is not a simple task where several meanings intersect and contradict each other; an example of this will be the existence of varying social, environmental and retail definitions attached to this term.
   a. Value chain
   b. Green marketing
   c. Market share
   d. SWOT analysis

13. _____ is an integrated communications-based process through which individuals and communities discover that existing and newly-identified needs and wants may be satisfied by the products and services of others.

Chapter 20. Public Policy Issues

_____ is defined by the American _____ Association as the activity, set of institutions, and processes for creating, communicating, delivering, and exchanging offerings that have value for customers, clients, partners, and society at large. The term developed from the original meaning which referred literally to going to market, as in shopping, or going to a market to buy or sell goods or services.

a. Customer relationship management
b. Disruptive technology
c. Market development
d. Marketing

14. A _____ is one scenario provided for evaluation by respondents in a Choice Experiment. Responses are collected and used to create a Choice Model. Respondents are usually provided with a series of differing _____s for evaluation.

a. Thurstone scale
b. Pairwise comparison
c. Computerized classification test
d. Choice Set

15. A _____ is a name or trademark connected with a product or producer. _____s have become increasingly important components of culture and the economy, now being described as 'cultural accessories and personal philosophies'.

Some people distinguish the psychological aspect of a _____ from the experiential aspect.

a. Brand extension
b. Brand awareness
c. Brand
d. Brand loyalty

16. _____ are legal property rights over creations of the mind, both artistic and commercial, and the corresponding fields of law. Under _____ law, owners are granted certain exclusive rights to a variety of intangible assets, such as musical, literary, and artistic works; ideas, discoveries and inventions; and words, phrases, symbols, and designs. Common types of _____ include copyrights, trademarks, patents, industrial design rights and trade secrets.

a. Intent
b. Unemployment Action Center
c. Equal Pay Act
d. Intellectual property

17. _____ plant, and equipment, is a term used in accountancy for assets and property which cannot easily be converted into cash. This can be compared with current assets such as cash or bank accounts, which are described as liquid assets. In most cases, only tangible assets are referred to as fixed.

   a. 28-hour day
   b. Fixed asset
   c. 33 Strategies of War
   d. 1990 Clean Air Act

18. In economics, a _____ exists when a specific individual or enterprise has sufficient control over a particular product or service to determine significantly the terms on which other individuals shall have access to it. Monopolies are thus characterized by a lack of economic competition for the good or service that they provide and a lack of viable substitute goods. The verb 'monopolize' refers to the process by which a firm gains persistently greater market share than what is expected under perfect competition.

   a. 28-hour day
   b. 33 Strategies of War
   c. 1990 Clean Air Act
   d. Monopoly

19. A _____ is a set of exclusive rights granted by a state to an inventor or his assignee for a limited period of time in exchange for a disclosure of an invention.

   The procedure for granting _____s, the requirements placed on the _____ee and the extent of the exclusive rights vary widely between countries according to national laws and international agreements. Typically, however, a _____ application must include one or more claims defining the invention which must be new, inventive, and useful or industrially applicable.

   a. Food, Drug, and Cosmetic Act
   b. Labor Management Reporting and Disclosure Act
   c. Federal Trade Commission Act
   d. Patent

20. _____ is one of the managerial functions like planning, organizing, staffing and directing. It is an important function because it helps to check the errors and to take the corrective action so that deviation from standards are minimized and stated goals of the organization are achieved in desired manner. According to modern concepts, _____ is a foreseeing action whereas earlier concept of _____ was used only when errors were detected. _____ in management means setting standards, measuring actual performance and taking corrective action.

a. Turnover
b. Control
c. Schedule of reinforcement
d. Decision tree pruning

21. An _____ is any party that makes an investment.

The term has taken on a specific meaning in finance to describe the particular types of people and companies that regularly purchase equity or debt securities for financial gain in exchange for funding an expanding company. Less frequently, the term is applied to parties who purchase real estate, currency, commodity derivatives, personal property, or other assets.

a. A Stake in the Outcome
b. A4e
c. Investor
d. AAAI

22. A _____, in the field of business and marketing, is a geographic region or demographic group used to gauge the viability of a product or service in the mass market prior to a wide scale roll-out. The criteria used to judge the acceptability of a _____ region or group include:

1. a population that is demographically similar to the proposed target market; and
2. relative isolation from densely populated media markets so that advertising to the test audience can be efficient and economical.

The _____ ideally aims to duplicate 'everything' - promotion and distribution as well as `product' - on a smaller scale. The technique replicates, typically in one area, what is planned to occur in a national launch; and the results are very carefully monitored, so that they can be extrapolated to projected national results. The `area' may be any one of the following:

- Television area

internet online test

- Test town
- Residential neighborhood
- Test site

Chapter 20. Public Policy Issues

A number of decisions have to be taken about any _____:

- Which _____?
- What is to be tested?
- How long a test?
- What are the success criteria?

The simple go or no-go decision, together with the related reduction of risk, is normally the main justification for the expense of _____s. At the same time, however, such _____s can be used to test specific elements of a new product's marketing mix; possibly the version of the product itself, the promotional message and media spend, the distribution channels and the price.

a. 33 Strategies of War
b. 28-hour day
c. 1990 Clean Air Act
d. Test market

23. _____ is a form of communication that typically attempts to persuade potential customers to purchase or to consume more of a particular brand of product or service. 'While now central to the contemporary global economy and the reproduction of global production networks, it is only quite recently that _____ has been more than a marginal influence on patterns of sales and production. The formation of modern _____ was intimately bound up with the emergence of new forms of monopoly capitalism around the end of the 19th and beginning of the 20th century as one element in corporate strategies to create, organize and where possible control markets, especially for mass produced consumer goods.
    a. Advertising
    b. A4e
    c. AAAI
    d. A Stake in the Outcome

24. A _____ is a professional who provides advice in a particular area of expertise such as management, accountancy, the environment, entertainment, technology, law , human resources, marketing, medicine, finance, economics, public affairs, communication, engineering, sound system design, graphic design, or waste management.

A _____ is usually an expert or a professional in a specific field and has a wide knowledge of the subject matter. A _____ usually works for a consultancy firm or is self-employed, and engages with multiple and changing clients.

Chapter 20. Public Policy Issues

a. Consultant
b. 1990 Clean Air Act
c. 33 Strategies of War
d. 28-hour day

25. Consumer market research is a form of applied sociology that concentrates on understanding the behaviours, whims and preferences, of consumers in a market-based economy, and aims to understand the effects and comparative success of marketing campaigns. The field of consumer _____ as a statistical science was pioneered by Arthur Nielsen with the founding of the ACNielsen Company in 1923 .

Thus _____ is the systematic and objective identification, collection, analysis, and dissemination of information for the purpose of assisting management in decision making related to the identification and solution of problems and opportunities in marketing.

a. Market analysis
b. 1990 Clean Air Act
c. Marketing research process
d. Marketing research

26. A _____ is a group of people or organizations sharing one or more characteristics that cause them to have similar product and/or service needs. A true _____ meets all of the following criteria: it is distinct from other segments (different segments have different needs), it is homogeneous within the segment (exhibits common needs); it responds similarly to a market stimulus, and it can be reached by a market intervention. The term is also used when consumers with identical product and/or service needs are divided up into groups so they can be charged different amounts.

a. Customer relationship management
b. Context analysis
c. Market segment
d. SWOT analysis

27. _____ is a strategic planning method that some organizations use to make flexible long-term plans. It is in large part an adaptation and generalization of classic methods used by military intelligence.

The original method was that a group of analysts would generate simulation games for policy makers. In business applications, the emphasis on gaming the behavior of opponents was reduced (shifting more toward a game against nature). At Royal Dutch/Shell for example, _____ was viewed as changing mindsets about the exogenous part of the world, prior to formulating specific strategies.

a. Time and attendance
b. Labour productivity
c. Scenario planning
d. Retroactive overtime

28. The term '_____' refers to the concept of collecting information and attempting to spot a pattern in the information. In some fields of study, the term '_____' has more formally-defined meanings.

In project management _____ is a mathematical technique that uses historical results to predict future outcome.

a. Stepwise regression
b. Regression analysis
c. Least squares
d. Trend analysis

29. The _____ captures an expanded spectrum of values and criteria for measuring organizational success: economic, ecological and social. With the ratification of the United Nations and ICLEI _____ standard for urban and community accounting in early 2007, this became the dominant approach to public sector full cost accounting. Similar UN standards apply to natural capital and human capital measurement to assist in measurements required by _____, e.g. the ecoBudget standard for reporting ecological footprint.

a. 33 Strategies of War
b. Triple bottom line
c. 1990 Clean Air Act
d. 28-hour day

30. _____ is a group creativity technique designed to generate a large number of ideas for the solution of a problem. The method was first popularized in the late 1930s by Alex Faickney Osborn in a book called Applied Imagination. Osborn proposed that groups could double their creative output with _____.

a. Affiliation
b. Abraham Harold Maslow
c. Brainstorming
d. Adam Smith

31. A _____ is a set of consistent ethic values (more specifically the personal and cultural values) and measures used for the purpose of ethical or ideological integrity. A well defined _____ is a moral code.

Fred Wenst>øp and Arild Myrmel have proposed a structure for corporate _____s that consists of three value categories. These are considered complementary and juxtaposed on the same level if illustrated graphically on for instance an organization's web page. The first value category is Core Values, which prescribe the attitude and character of an organization, and are often found in sections on Code of conduct on its web page. The philosophical antecedents of these values are Virtue ethics, which is often attributed to Aristotle. Protected Values are protected through rules, standards and certifications. They are often concerned with areas such as health, environment and safety. The third category, Created Values, is the values that stakeholders, including the shareholders expect in return for their contributions to the firm. These values are subject to trade-off by decision-makers or bargaining processes. This process is explained further in Stakeholder theory.

a. 1990 Clean Air Act
b. Value system
c. 28-hour day
d. 33 Strategies of War

32. A _____ is a written document that details the necessary actions to achieve one or more marketing objectives. It can be for a product or service, a brand, or a product line. _____s cover between one and five years.
a. Marketing plan
b. Disruptive technology
c. Market development
d. Marketing strategy

ANSWER KEY

Chapter 1
1. c 2. a 3. d 4. b 5. c 6. b 7. d 8. a 9. b 10. b
11. d 12. a 13. d 14. d 15. d 16. a 17. a 18. b 19. a 20. a
21. c 22. d 23. d 24. c 25. c

Chapter 2
1. b 2. c 3. a 4. c 5. d 6. d 7. d 8. d 9. d 10. c
11. c 12. d 13. d 14. d 15. c 16. a 17. d 18. c 19. a 20. b
21. c 22. c 23. d 24. d 25. b

Chapter 3
1. b 2. b 3. d 4. b 5. d 6. d 7. d 8. c 9. b 10. d
11. a 12. d 13. a 14. d 15. d 16. d 17. c 18. d 19. d 20. b
21. d 22. a

Chapter 4
1. d 2. a 3. c 4. a 5. d 6. b 7. a 8. d 9. b 10. d
11. c 12. d 13. d 14. a

Chapter 5
1. d 2. d 3. d 4. a 5. d 6. d 7. d 8. d 9. b

Chapter 6
1. d 2. b 3. a 4. c 5. c 6. c 7. d 8. a

Chapter 7
1. a 2. b 3. a 4. c 5. b 6. c 7. a 8. d 9. c

Chapter 8
1. d 2. d 3. a 4. d 5. a 6. c 7. d 8. d 9. d 10. a
11. d 12. c 13. c

Chapter 9
1. a 2. d 3. a 4. d 5. a 6. d 7. d 8. a 9. d 10. b
11. a 12. d

Chapter 10
1. b 2. c 3. d 4. d 5. c 6. a 7. d 8. d

Chapter 11
1. d 2. d 3. d 4. d 5. d 6. d 7. a 8. d 9. d 10. d
11. d 12. d 13. b 14. d 15. d 16. b 17. d 18. b 19. c

Chapter 12
1. b 2. d 3. d 4. a 5. a 6. d 7. b 8. d 9. d 10. d

ANSWER KEY

Chapter 13
1. b   2. d   3. d   4. b   5. d   6. b   7. d   8. c   9. b   10. c
11. b   12. d   13. d   14. b

Chapter 14
1. d   2. d   3. d   4. d   5. b   6. c   7. c   8. c   9. d   10. b
11. c   12. b   13. d   14. d   15. b   16. c   17. d   18. a   19. d   20. a
21. d   22. d   23. a   24. b

Chapter 15
1. c   2. d   3. d   4. d   5. d   6. c   7. b   8. d   9. d   10. d

Chapter 16
1. d   2. d   3. d   4. d   5. d   6. d   7. b   8. a   9. d   10. d
11. b   12. d   13. b   14. d   15. b   16. d   17. d   18. d   19. a   20. d
21. d   22. d   23. a   24. d   25. d   26. b   27. d   28. a

Chapter 17
1. a   2. c   3. d   4. b   5. d   6. d   7. b

Chapter 18
1. c   2. d   3. d   4. a   5. c   6. d   7. d   8. d   9. d   10. c
11. c   12. c   13. d   14. b

Chapter 19
1. a   2. c   3. d   4. b   5. a   6. d   7. d

Chapter 20
1. b   2. b   3. d   4. d   5. d   6. d   7. d   8. c   9. d   10. d
11. d   12. b   13. d   14. d   15. c   16. d   17. b   18. d   19. d   20. b
21. c   22. d   23. a   24. a   25. d   26. c   27. c   28. d   29. b   30. c
31. b   32. a

www.ingramcontent.com/pod-product-compliance
Lightning Source LLC
Chambersburg PA
CBHW082052230426
43670CB00016B/2860